A LIFE

BEYOND

WORDS

A Life Beyond Words:
A family's journey through hardship and loss
to the joy of unspoken possibilities

2024 YTGMedia Co. Press Trade Paperback Edition.
Copyright © 2024 Susan Baker

Published in Canada, for Global Distribution by YTGMedia Co.
www.ygtmedia.co
For more information email: info@ygtmedia.co

ISBN trade paperback: 978-1-998754-75-5
eBook: 978-1-998754-76-2

To order additional copies of this book:
info@ygtmedia.co

Author Photography: Brianna Roye, IG: @briannablank
Cover Photo: Kari Shea on Unsplash

A LIFE BEYOND WORDS

*A family's journey through hardship and loss
to the joy of unspoken possibilities*

SUSAN BAKER

AUTHOR OF THE BLOG LIFE, LOVE & AUTISM

To my three beautiful children,

Andrew, James, and Abby,

for teaching me everything.

And to Stuart,

for walking with me through this life.

TO YOU

To the mother of a child with exceptional needs:

Yes, *all of our children have needs* and *all of our children are exceptional*–these are *human* needs–but you know what I mean. Your child has extra needs, "special" needs, unique needs. I see you; I know what that entails. And I know you can do this. You can walk this path. You will be okay. Your child will be okay too.

To the mother who has lost a child:

There are no words except *you are not alone.*

And to the mother parenting an exceptional sibling:

You have the love and patience and time required for them too. You do. They know this. They know they are loved, even when it seems unavailable. There is love there.

You are doing enough.
You are enough.
Keep showing up.

Love,
Susan

INTRODUCTION

I am a storyteller. I write stories using words that create a feeling, paint a picture, or share a window into an otherwise hard-to-describe experience. It was not difficult to write this story, our story, but the story had to unfold. It took many years. It was written as we journeyed through this life.

If you had told me this would be my story, I'm not sure I would have believed you:

You will have three children. Three beautiful beings. Three opportunities for growth.

You will lose one: a newborn baby boy. He will die in your arms. Your heart will shatter, but in that pile of brokenness, you will find pieces of yourself you have never seen before.

You will have one who doesn't speak. One who doesn't come with a guide or with answers—not in the way you expect. He will walk a unique path and be your teacher. You will learn everything you need to know along the way.

You will have a third—a gift, pure joy. She will show you there is light after dark.

As a mother, you will be stripped down to your bare bones—raw, torn, broken. You will fall and wonder if you will ever get up again.

All three will teach you lessons beyond this world. They will teach you your strength, your character, and your courage.

And you will get up. You will rise beyond the realm of what you ever thought possible for yourself.

This will be your life—the life meant for you.

We all have a story. We have events that shape us, that build us up, tear us down, and re-create us into who we are meant to become. These simple, spectacular, sometimes painful moments create the story of a life that is ours.

Our stories nourish the soul in all of us. It is in vulnerably sharing our story that we realize we are not alone.

Our stories matter.

Our stories, in fact, heal.

This is my story—a story of perseverance, of courage, of trust, and of letting go. What was once a story of loss became a story of strength. One of despair became one of hope. And what could have been one of giving up became one of purpose, joy, and infinite potential.

This is the story of a life beyond words.

PART I: AWARENESS

"MY GOAL IN LIFE
IS TO SHOW UP AS I AM;
THAT IS ENOUGH,
AS IT IS FOR ALL OF US."

-ANDREW

CHAPTER 1

I remember playing "house" as a little girl in the basement of our suburban middle-class family home. I was the mom. Even if I was playing with my sister, or a friend from down the street, I was the mother. I always had three babies. I would dress up my dolls in little clothes, feed them in their little chairs, and give them naps in their little beds. I named them, cared for them, and played with them. Not that I was particularly maternal, but I was loyal. When my little brother came along, I played "family" with *him*. I dressed him up in doll clothes, pushed him around in a doll stroller, and pretended to feed him. Not unlike many children, I acted out the life I envisioned for myself. Yes, I wanted to be a teacher, or a cashier, and later, a neuroscientist or a psychologist, but something in me knew I would always be a mother. Perhaps I knew, too, that I would be the mother to three children.

My family life was typical. My dad, an engineer, met my mom, an office administrator, through work. They were married seven years before they had children. I was born in Winnipeg, Manitoba. My sister, Jayne, was born shortly thereafter in Vancouver, British Columbia. After yet another transfer, my parents settled in Markham, Ontario, a developing suburb of Toronto, where they had my brother, John. We lived there in that family home until each of us were either married or living on our own, a span of close to thirty years.

Our home was full of laughter, conversation, music, and playfulness, as well as arguments, tension, and complex family dynamics. In many ways, it was "the norm": I had a mom and a dad, two siblings, and eventually, a dog named Rex. It also felt unique. Both my parents had grown up poor, in underprivileged European immigrant families with stories of hard times and bare-boned Christmases. My father was a success story in his family, attending university and earning a salaried job at an established and expanding corporation. My mother dedicated herself to raising her children, right up until I was in high school when she began working part-time as an administrator at our local Catholic church parish (which we attended regularly).

We were a close family. Breaking generations of trauma and misfortune, my parents worked hard at their relationship, at communication, and at raising healthy children. Eventually, they worked hard on themselves too. Mom immersed herself in personal growth and spirituality, while Dad steadily uncovered himself and thereby, his relationship with his children. I watched my parents crumble and rebuild themselves as individuals and as a couple over many years. Mom had an unwavering strength and faith in God and life. Dad had a simple outlook and an abundant love for his children. Both were learning how to live as healthy individuals while also learning how to raise a family through values of love, respect, gratitude, forgiveness, and grace. I grew up very attached, caring deeply for my siblings. We argued and bickered, but there was mostly great love and friendship there, especially as we grew older. We faced many challenges as a family and always came through them with love.

What I learned growing up was that you *face* adversity, you don't run from it. You confront hard emotions, hard situations, and hard people with love and integrity. Over time, the hard becomes easier. You speak up. You use your "God-given voice," my mom would say, to make change, to make things right. You advocate for your needs and the needs of others.

Ours was a family that talked about emotions and shared about our day. My upbringing was foundational. It wasn't "perfect," but it was perfect in its example of what it looked like to experience love and loss, hardship and growth—in relationships and in being human.

I have always loved life. My parents called it a zest, an enthusiastic and earnest desire to experience life and always do my best. I had friends, did well in school, played sports, and danced. I wasn't necessarily an extrovert, but I was confident enough to try out for teams, join councils and clubs, and attend overnight summer camp. I was bright, analytical, and tenacious.

In the same breath, I always felt anxious. From the time I was a little girl I felt an unsettled feeling, like an undercurrent, a default way of *being*. Always needing to "get it right," I would spend hours deliberating a decision or procrastinating on a project. At home, wanting everything to *be okay*, I would check in on Mom's mood or Dad's availability. I sought security and could achieve this by trying to be perfect. I learned in time that part of my anxiety was actually excitement (with a bit of trepidation). I realized I could turn my fear into courage: "Feel the fear and do it anyway," my parents would say.

I grew up with personal tools. I was encouraged to identify my feelings, to journal, to pray. My mother brought the wisdom of The Enneagram, a nine-type personality system rooted in psychology and spirituality, into our lives. At first we balked, resisting the identification as one type, seeing it as a reduction of who we were. Over time, I grew to embrace The Enneagram and my type ("the Six": fearful yet courageous, fiercely loyal and dogmatic, often skeptical of convention) as a way of fully stepping into who I was, finding validation in the relatable challenges and vision in the way of growth. It informed the lens through which I viewed life, positively impacting my relationships and myself.

From a young age I felt a deep connection to what I knew to be "Spirit" or "Source"—a divine energy and aspect within my being and all of creation. Growing up, we called it God—the classic, omnipresent, grandfatherly figure "up above." Over the years, this image evolved for me. It included what I felt in the love for my family, the awe I experienced in nature, and the beauty I saw in the world around me, including humanity itself. I recognized all people as being created in the image and likeness of a magnificent entity, a source of abundant love, intention, and purpose. One that made no mistakes. I called it life.

This was who I was. A bright, happy girl who loved life, learning, and the richness that came through self-reflection. It is still who I am.

***

At fifteen, I became a vegetarian. Not typically newsworthy, but in this story, this event is pivotal. This single decision would completely steer the course of my life: my health, my career, and the way I would raise my children. All because I refused pork chops for dinner one night. I had done a fetal pig dissection in biology class. It was the first time I had ever made a "farm to plate" food connection. I felt uneasy, ate a peanut butter sandwich instead, and never looked back. Not for fifteen years.

I was raised on a typical North American diet of meat and potatoes. Other vegetables were accessories: frozen corn or peas, maybe sautéed carrots. This is what Mom knew, so when I omitted meat, her only suggestions for protein were peanut butter (the kind with added sugar and processed oils) and cheese (and it would be years before I would learn that I was lactose intolerant). I gained weight, had terrible digestive issues, and my seasonal allergies got worse.

While at university, I became friends with people who were into camping, mountain biking, and vegetarianism. They taught me about hummus (from chickpeas), tofu (from soybeans), natural peanut butter (made only with peanuts), and other forms of vegetarian protein. I felt better and had more energy.

Then two significant occurrences took place. My mother started seeing a functional medical doctor who, over a period of time, turned her health around through natural medicine. She learned about natural foods and therapeutic supplements. She called me at school one day and said, "Susan, I think our entire family is lactose intolerant. Go a week without cheese and see what happens." And I did, and my health changed. I was no longer gassy and bloated, but more so, it was the first time I noted how food could make me feel.

Then later, while working post-university, I attended a vegetarian food festival in Toronto. How enlightening to hang out with hundreds of other people who identified with a similar lifestyle to my own. (They liked veggie burgers and sweet potato fries too!) As I walked by the various booths, with everything from natural soap to vegan bacon, I stalled at one particular table with a banner that claimed Food Is Medicine. The science behind food (and perhaps why I was feeling so much better) spoke to me. I picked up the brochure on display at the table and felt an overwhelming pull to learn more. The brochure was for a holistic nutrition college in Toronto. Within days (which was quick decision-making for me), I was registered in their one-year holistic nutrition diploma program. I had just finished a four-year bachelor's degree in science and, with no hesitation, was signing up for more school.

Learning about holistic health completely changed my life. Within a year of the program, I was a different person on all levels: physically, mentally, and spiritually. My health improved as my lifestyle shifted. I went from eating tubs of jujubes to bowls of kale salad. I had great energy, I was no longer anemic and allergic, and I felt purpose in my life. So impacted by this shift, I decided I had to share it with others. This passion became my career, which brought with it a community of like-minded mentors and friends.

Upon graduation, I accepted an opportunity to practice nutrition at a naturopathic health clinic located, coincidentally, around the corner from my family home. There, I met other holistic health practitioners who became significant influences on my career, including an energy therapist named Jade. Jade would become one of my closest friends.

I worked 'round the clock, getting my nutrition business off the ground, consulting, presenting corporate seminars, and teaching at the nutrition college I had attended. Eventually, I worked shifts at a popular health food store. I loved it *and* I could get a discount on all the food and supplements I had become accustomed to buying.

I remained vegetarian for fifteen years, right up until halfway through my pregnancy with my first child. One morning I just woke up and said, "I need to start eating meat." It felt like a direct message from my body. With no idea how to shop for (or cook) it, I walked into the health food store and asked for a pound of organic ground beef. I went home, looked up a recipe for chili, and had that for dinner. After fifteen years of vegetarianism, at the age of thirty, I was eating meat again.

In the months and years that followed my child's autism diagnosis, I often wondered, Was it something I did? Was it the years of being vegetarian? Was I somehow deficient in vital nutrients essential for a healthy child? Was my digestion and the health of my gut not healthy enough? Was it the stress of working multiple jobs while I was pregnant? Was it that one drink I had late in my pregnancy? Should I have done something different? More cleansing? Less cleansing? More protein? Less fried tempura (which I craved)? I would always wonder.

Food and health had become the whole of who I was. I was a different person, a healthier version, because of it. It set the trajectory for all that was to come.

***

I met Stuart on his twenty-first birthday. My longtime childhood friend, Fiona, introduced us. Her family was friends with Stuart's family, and when she felt obliged to attend his twenty-first birthday celebration, I went along. I was enamored by Stuart's vibrance and humor, not to mention that he wore strappy leather sandals and played guitar.

Spending time with Stuart felt different. I'd had other boyfriends, but with Stuart, time felt natural and easy. I could fully be myself. We laughed a lot and had similar values and mutual interests. We were smitten. We went to concerts, parties, and poetry nights. We hung out at each other's homes and spent time with each other's families. Initially, we maintained a long-distance relationship while I was at university, albeit less than a two-hour drive away. As a couple, we were independent yet deeply connected. I was there when he landed his first real job, when he started his career in finance, and when he scrimped and saved to put money down on his first house. Stuart was there when

I went to school to study holistic nutrition and later, to become a certified teacher. He watched as I worked four jobs as a newly graduated holistic health entrepreneur.

Our relationship was serious and real and we both knew it. We worked hard, had fun, and traveled when we could, including taking a road trip across North America. Within five years we were engaged. Stuart proposed at sunset on a camping trip, shaking and tripping over his words. I accepted, nervous and elated. At twenty-six, we were married. Young and healthy, we had our whole lives ahead of us. We were committed and ready to live together through love, mutual respect, growth, and challenge.

We were in love, but our first year of married life was not easy. Under financial strain, our arguments felt amplified. Our busy work schedules and precarious finances left us on edge. Eventually, Stuart was able to advance his career such that we had a more meaningful income on which to rely. Within six months of being married, we moved from Stuart's starter home into a townhouse of our own, just around the corner and within thirty minutes of both our families.

I loved my work—delivering nutrition seminars in corporations and teaching at the holistic nutrition college lit me up. I had learned that speaking was my passion; I loved using my voice to inspire others. I mentored hundreds of nutrition graduates, hosting workshops out of my home. I organized monthly networking meetings for fellow holistic nutritionists at our local library, featuring a different speaker every month.

Life felt busy and strained, but overall, Stuart and I were happy. In fact, we were a lot of fun.

We knew we wanted to have children. When we were dating, we freely talked about having kids, how many we'd have, and what we'd name them. So carefree and naive. After a few years of being married, we felt ready for that next responsibility. At thirty years old, with what seemed like just a thought, we were pregnant. Imagine that. We were going to have a baby! We were thrilled.

We waited until the first-trimester ultrasound, which confirmed a heartbeat, and then gleefully shared our news. We told everyone. Ours was the first pregnancy in our family, the first grandchild, the first niece or nephew, the first baby. Even among our group of friends, ours was one of the first.

Fiercely committed to all things natural (and by this point, not one for medical interventions), we did not do any prenatal tests or additional ultrasounds beyond confirming the pregnancy. We enlisted the care of a team of midwives who monitored our pregnancy and guided our path.

I did "all the right things": I took all the right supplements and ate all the right foods. I did prenatal yoga, moved my body, and practiced mindfulness and relaxation. I was confident in my approach and was feeling supported, prepared, and excited. My pregnancy was textbook. I gained a perfect amount of weight and felt tired only in my first trimester. I was glowing. I prepared an all-natural labor and delivery kit for the hospital: homeopathics to support contractions, natural pain relief, and organic blankets for the baby. I was fully invested.

One day toward the end of the pregnancy, I was struck by an overwhelming sense of love. I was connecting to this child in a way that seemed almost selfish, gaining insight into *my* life and wisdom from my higher self. On some level, I knew this child would be unique, maybe even unconventional. I had a feeling he'd lead me to learning unconditional love. I shared this with Stuart, though I couldn't quite explain it: "I don't know—like maybe he won't *fit the mold* somehow." I didn't know about autism. I knew, though, this child would be *different*. That day I knew my child's role would be to teach me how to love beyond differences, to walk the path less taken, and ultimately, to learn to let go. This child would teach me how to surrender to the process of life.

It's as though there were signs, like a foreshadowing, leading me into life with this child.

I attended my first silent retreat when I was eight months pregnant. A *silent* retreat. It had been recommended to me by a holistic health friend as a way to create calm and centering before the birth. Yes, I loved to speak, but I remember thinking, *How hard can it be?* Now I can see why I was meant to be there: I learned what being in total silence was like. I learned to communicate without words. I learned to *just be*. I had never experienced this before. The anxiety within me that I had come to know so well dissipated with this newfound awareness. I learned the practice of observation, breath, and stillness. Of course, I had no idea my whole life would become this.

At that same time, I received the summer issue of an alternative-thinking magazine—actually just days before Andrew was born. Called the *Silence* issue, the entire issue was dedicated to articles about silence, stillness, and nature. I flipped through it, not paying much attention to the depth of its content, preoccu pied by the imminent arrival of my baby. But I kept it. I recycled all other issues (in my pre-baby nesting phase) but kept that one. I've read it since, in a whole new light. I must have known it's what I would need.

***

Andrew was born in the middle of the night on a Tuesday in June. He came when he was ready. He was a week overdue, and

I'd had spicy curry for dinner and gone for a long walk with Stu before heading to bed. After feeling the urge to pee, I ran to the toilet when water started trickling down my leg. It smelled like saline; my waters had broken. My heart raced. This was it! We were excited and nervous. I went back to bed to lie down, but within minutes I felt my first contraction. It was happening.

Twenty minutes later, my contractions were five minutes apart and very strong. We grabbed our bags, jumped (waddled!) into the car, and sped to the hospital, texting our midwife along the way. I was in pain. It all became a blur.

We arrived at the hospital and had only been admitted a mere thirty minutes prior when the medical team urgently suggested I move to a delivery room. My contractions were increasing steadily. Delivery was imminent. Wanting a natural labor, I resisted until I could no longer bear the pain, then finally asked for an epidural. As the doctor prepared the injection, our midwife did a quick check of my cervix only to notice that I was already nine centimeters dilated. No wonder the pain was so intense! We abandoned the epidural and prepared to push. What followed was an absolute whirlwind, one of the most intense physical and mental experiences of my life. My labor lasted three hours, with a mere twenty-minute pause before active pushing began. Andrew was delivered in just under thirty minutes. Stuart and I were shaking yet enthralled. The whole process was incredible.

Andrew was born, nine pounds and five ounces, at 3:49 a.m. He was full and fleshy with bright pink skin and a beautiful face. I marveled at how gorgeous he was. Although he arrived with vigor, he arrived peaceful and serene. He latched right away, the innate ability to breastfeed happening so naturally. We were home in no time, keen and scared.

Although my recovery was difficult, I kept with my desire to be drug-free—not even a Tylenol for the pain. I was an idealist. I wanted as pure a start to life as possible for my child. It continued right through Andrew's infancy.

Andrew was breastfed for eighteen months. We introduced solid foods at six months and included only vegetables and fruit (mostly organic and home-prepared). Grains were delayed as I had learned that introducing them too soon could cause a "leaky gut," leading to potential allergies and other health issues later on. We gave Andrew probiotics (good bacteria for the gut), and as he grew, he drank only water and breastmilk and continued to eat only healthy, whole foods. No sugar, no wheat, no cow's dairy.

He received no vaccinations. Although both Stuart and I were vaccinated as infants, we agreed on a delayed vaccination schedule based on my understanding of an infant's permeable gut lining and immature immune system and the related concerns. To this day, Andrew is unvaccinated. Although I do believe the stories of parents who have watched their child medically regress after receiving one (or more) of the vaccines in the standard childhood immunization schedule, often noted and medically documented by their child's pediatrician, this was not the case with Andrew. We can say with certainty, he was who he was from the beginning. Any vaccine toxicity potentially related to his development would have come through me, in utero.

As an infant, Andrew didn't have screen time or play with electronic toys. He spent plenty of time outside in nature, in fresh air. We played gentle music and honored nap times and bedtimes. We were playful, but I was always slightly anxious. If there was a right way to do it, I felt I needed to be on top of it. Only there was no right way. I would learn that eventually.

He was a sensitive baby, often needing long periods of rocking or swaying to fall asleep, even just for a nap. He was healthy and growing rapidly, though I always felt that he wasn't getting *enough*. He seemed agitated and restless. Was I not producing enough milk? Based on his size, that didn't appear to be the case; this kid was getting the cream! I nursed him constantly. Even when I went back to teaching, I pumped milk in the bathroom stalls so I could keep up my supply and have plenty for when I left Andrew with Stuart or a grandparent. He never had formula, just breastmilk and, eventually, solid food. His bowel movements were regular; though, as a toddler, they had a putrid smell–different from what I thought was normal. There were no gastro issues, no complications to be concerned about, but I took note of the smell and consistency. It was important to me as a holistic nutritionist to gain all insight from a client's digestive symptoms. After all, that was my specialty and this was my child.

***

To me, Andrew was perfect and wondrous and I didn't know any different. Except that he was; he was *different*.

By the time he was two, we were noticing atypical development. Andrew had walked at one but had never mastered crawling. We thought it was hilarious the way he dragged one leg across the floor, but again, I took note. He talked at two, but it was mostly word approximations. We were so eager to hear him say "Mama" and "Dada" that we delighted in every sound, every attempt, he made.

By age two and a half, though, those sounds had all but diminished. I worried that the double dose of antibiotics he had been given for back-to-back ear infections at the age of two (something he was not prone to but had shown up directly after I introduced homemade organic yogurt), or his bout with pneumonia, had set him back. Part of me wondered if his regression had anything to do with a traumatic event our family had just experienced right at this pivotal stage of Andrew's development. Part of me will always wonder.

"He'll be a late talker," people said to put our minds at ease.

He studied everything: little crinkly bags, the way the sunlight shone through a window, how the pages of a book sounded at his ear.

"He'll be a scientist," they said. He was serious and studious and rarely needed adult interaction.

"You were just like that!" my mom said.

And I was. We are our children—we see ourselves in our children—and I loved all of who I saw in Andrew. But I wondered, Was there something? Was he okay? Was he just different? A bit like me? A bit like Grandma or Poppa? Was I just being hypervigilant? Or was something going on?

I wanted to believe that Andrew was just fine. Besides, he was content. He showed affection and made eye contact but seemed easily overwhelmed and more frustrated and sensitive than other children. He showed very little interest in being with other kids, especially younger ones. "Oh, they parallel play at this age," people said to us. And we were okay with that.

I tried not to compare. More differences became apparent, and over time, Andrew looked less and less like the other kids. He was the child at the parent-and-tot group who pushed the markers around on the floor and watched them bounce down the steps instead of using them to color. I was only slightly embarrassed seeing the perplexed faces of other parents who would watch Andrew sit silently, contently, on his own, while their children played noisily with trucks and dolls and kitchen sets, modeling "appropriate imitation play" and learning how to take turns. Not Andrew. He was *different*.

He could sit for hours, flipping through the pages of a book or magazine. He watched the wind rustling in the trees outside. He loved *sound*: the sound of a rippling stream, the sound of tissue paper by his ear, the sound of music or singing. We imagined he could hear things we couldn't hear, things in his world, not ours. I watched him on our walks, so taken by the world around him. We never rushed. We would stand by the edge of a riverbank, watching the water roll over the fallen trees, listening. He would listen to the wind in the leaves of the trees, way up in the sky, fluttering and clapping. Andrew loved it. Smiling, his little curls blowing in the breeze, he would turn away, then turn back laughing, and I imagined he heard a symphony. He seemed so enamored by nature. He was happiest outside, so at peace. It was as though his apparent uniqueness was matched by the uniqueness of each leaf, each blade of grass, each tree. It was like he was at home.

Exceptional as he was, Stuart and I were definitely concerned. This put strain on our marriage. While I wanted to support Andrew's individuality, Stuart raised questions about Andrew's behavior. Did this mean we weren't aligned in how we were to raise our kids? Watching our firstborn child not develop according to textbook, not hitting milestones, was distracting and confusing. Tensions mounted. We felt hopeful as a couple, hopeful about our life and our future as a family, but we had no idea where to go with our concerns.

Then one day we were pregnant. Surprised and thrilled, we put our worries about Andrew's development on hold for the moment. It wouldn't be long before we would need to look at them again, but not before our strength was tested. As a couple, we were in for the trial of our life.

"BECOMING A MOTHER,
YOU LEARN
IT'S ALL ABOUT LOVE."

-SUSAN

CHAPTER 2

This new pregnancy felt exciting. It held the vision we had of completing our family. It brought joy and a newfound focus. I was delighted. *What a gift to be able to conceive. How incredible that the human body is able to create new life. Will it be a girl? Another boy?*

We were due at the end of September. Stuart and I envisioned a gorgeous fall day with a new baby and a toddler in tow. Everyone was excited—our parents, our siblings, our friends. Life was going just as we imagined. Certainly, I was physically tired from having to take care of a toddler, but first-trimester fatigue was expected.

Andrew would be two when his brother or sister was born. Unsure of Andrew's awareness around this exciting family development, we spoke about it minimally with him. Yes, I put his chubby little hands on my growing belly and introduced him to his little brother or sister, but beyond that he seemed to pay little interest. He didn't ask questions (he still couldn't speak), nor did he seem interested in the "big brother" books and stories we would tell. I remember thinking, *What will Andrew be like as an older brother? Will he share toys? Will they get along?* I imagined him gentle, caring, and connected. He was like an old soul within our family. I pictured them becoming good friends. We imagined ourselves, Stuart and me, sitting on the front step of our home watching our little family grow up. I didn't picture what happened next.

I remember exactly where I was sitting when our midwife told me the news. There for the results of our second-trimester anatomical scan, I expected this routine ultrasound would confirm a healthy anatomy and determine the sex of the baby (which we would leave as a surprise until the birth). Stuart was at work. In my mind, this was like any other medical appointment: a standard review of normal results and then I'd be on my way. But the look on the midwife's face said something different. Her face was revealing—she was somber, and as she pulled out my file, I could tell something wasn't right. I felt irritated and confused.

When I recount this moment, my perspective is from above. I see myself sitting in the appointment room watching as the midwife enters to review the results of my mid-term ultrasound. I watch as my brow furrows and my smile fades when she reads from my chart. I see my hand trembling as I reach for the phone to call Stuart. Then the vision fades. The rest is a blur.

"I'm sorry . . . " she says, her voice trailing off.

She was an intern, a student of midwifery, and not our midwife. She was clearly uncomfortable in having to deliver the news. Results like this would be shocking to anyone. She was on her own with no clinical supervisor to guide her with this catastrophic report.

I look at her, disgruntled and bewildered. "Pardon?"

"I'm sorry, but your baby . . . there are some concerns . . . you will need to be referred to a high-risk pregnancy clinic . . . we can't take care of you here . . . your baby . . . there is a developmental abnormality . . . I'm so sorry . . . so sorry. Do you want to call your husband? Is he available? You might want to call him."

"Pardon?" My eyes wide, face burning hot, hands like ice. "Pardon? You want me to call my husband? Sorry, because why?

I don't understand. You're being vague and confusing. Is there a problem? You're saying there's a problem with the baby? You need to be more clear. I don't know what you're trying to say." I turn away, my voice tense.

I call Stuart at work. My throat is tight. I feel sick.

"Hi, Stuart. I'm with the midwife—not our midwife, a different one—she's trying to give me the results . . . it's confusing . . . apparently there is a problem . . . with the baby."

I can't remember what happened next. Everything went numb. Perhaps our brain does that to protect our heart.

***

Our baby was a boy. We learned this accidentally after an ultrasound with a urologist who identified a problem with one of our baby's kidneys. Our baby boy's anatomy was directly connected to why we were there, why the pregnancy was deemed "high risk." We had been referred to a high-risk pregnancy unit in one of Toronto's foremost obstetric hospitals, Mount Sinai. We were to have biweekly ultrasounds to monitor the health and development of the baby, particularly his underdeveloped kidney.

The urologist explained why my expanding belly was relatively small at this stage of the pregnancy (about six months). Due to the baby's smaller kidney, our baby was producing less urine, which, in turn, meant that the amniotic sac was less "full." (It is the production and excretion of urine by the baby that fills the amniotic sac.) Subsequently, these significantly lower amniotic fluid levels were a potential concern for prenatal lung development as the baby is required to "breathe" the amniotic fluid through its developing lungs for nourishment and growth of the lung tissue itself. Over the weeks, all of this would be assessed and monitored.

Our baby was also at a very high risk of complications at birth. If I made it full-term without difficulty or loss, there would surely be medical interventions and surgeries required. Stuart joined me in the first few visits to the high-risk unit, including one appointment of tremendous importance regarding the potential complications. Called "genetic counseling," the two of us sat together facing an unemotional clinician in a small, crowded room, listening to medical terminology and prenatal prognoses, most of which just sounded like white noise. I felt fortunate to have a science background. Stuart felt overwhelmed.

A long list of complications, scenarios, and outcomes were given, including miscarriage at any point and death at birth. There was a chance that our baby's one healthy kidney could do the work of two, but likely not well; he would need a kidney transplant, or certainly dialysis and other supports. More likely than any of this, though, was that our baby would be "incompatible with life."

The prenatal counselor paused and looked at us. "You need to know that you have options." We felt confused. "You do not need to continue with this pregnancy." I felt a heavy weight, like a boulder, in my stomach. I listened as the prenatal counselor continued: "You can terminate. You have medical reasons to consider this." I wanted to throw up. Stuart looked pale. "You may need time to think about it and discuss this as a couple."

I had a flashback to the time when I was a little girl playing house. How could I have ever imagined this? That my dream of being a mother would include this scenario: choose to live in hope but endure medical risk, or choose to end your child's life.

My head was spinning.

"Yes, we will need more time." Stuart and I got up and left the tiny hospital consultation room. We walked blankly out of the building into the hustling busy downtown street. We hardly spoke, but in the few short utterances we shared, our decision was made. We were in this together.

We had been given options for our child. We chose to see where fate (or, I believed, faith) would take us, even if it meant kidney transplants, infant dialysis, and a childhood full of visits with doctors. We would take our chances. And if dying was his fate, his soul's path, we would rather it be by his determination, not ours. We would put it in the hands of something greater than us. I trusted that we, too, would be held.

Some would disagree with us on this decision. Was this selfish? Were we delusional? Were we hurting our baby? Knowingly risking our child's start to life? Potentially subjecting our child to a life of intervention, complication, and unknown fate? We were solid in our conviction. For us, there was no other path.

Every two weeks I delighted in seeing our baby boy's sonogram. I prayed that his kidney would grow or that he was producing more urine, neither of which was typically the case. The staff at Mount Sinai's high-risk pregnancy unit were professional and kind. They understood the vulnerability of each patient in their care. There were women there at all stages: anxious early days, optimistic mid-stage like me, or grieving the late-stage loss of their complicated baby. It was both hopeful and awful being there.

That summer was a haze of medical appointments and follow-ups. I did my best to take care of myself while also balancing life with a toddler. Stuart was transitioning into a new role at his work, one that was both promising for his career and the future of our family but also very time-consuming.

I had found a home daycare nearby for Andrew, part-time, to give him a chance to be with children his age in a low-stress environment. I would drop him off, go down to the high-risk pregnancy unit for an ultrasound or follow-up, and be back in time to pick him up. Andrew managed there, enjoying time outside in the provider's tiny backyard, but he still wasn't showing much interest in the other children who attended.

We watched as Andrew's interests became more obscure. He would line up wooden blocks around the table edge. He could spin his set of multicolored plastic cups on the floor in front of him for minutes on end. We became more aware of the way he engaged with his environment, toddling around our forested backyard staring at the trees, picking up pine cones and listening to them at his ear, or laughing while chasing a leaf pile. He was so marvelous to watch. No doubt his world was different to ours. This was becoming more apparent. He was two, at the time.

We sought joy through all the confusion and worry. We floated around baby names: Ben, Roger, James, Ethan. We readied the baby's room, a blend of new and previously loved items from Andrew's time as an infant. We saw family and entertained friends, some of whom were pregnant at the same time as I was. Around the pool in our backyard, in our bathing suits, we observed how much bigger my friend's belly was than mine, laughing at the preciousness of this time and the vulnerability of it all. I held steady to my belief that all would be okay. This is what I truly believed.

By the end of the summer, with only minimal improvement in our baby's physiology, it was suggested that we schedule a planned induction and delivery at thirty-eight weeks. Medically considered full-term, the specialists could then begin to intervene, assess risk, and determine a treatment plan. His birth date was set: September 23. A day we would never forget.

In hindsight, I have wondered what would have happened had we not had that five-month ultrasound. What if I had done only the first-trimester ultrasound, like I had done with Andrew, confirming the heartbeat. (And only a second ultrasound when Andrew was a week overdue.) I comprehend that the second-trimester anatomical scan is routine and is for these exact situations. I have always just wondered. Would the trajectory have been different? It wouldn't have changed my pregnancy except that I wouldn't have had all the medical appointments, and all the anxiety and worry. Did it change our baby's birth circumstance? Knowing he was high risk, did it improve his outcome at birth? It was supposed to. In fact, everyone was hopeful. Yes, all possible scenarios were outlined during our prenatal counseling session, but to this day, I just wonder. What if I had gone into natural labor and birthed our baby in the hospital under "normal" circumstances? Would he have lived an hour? A day? Only minutes?

What would have happened had we not known?

We wouldn't have known James.

"LOVE IS MORE THAN
ANYTHING ELSE.
IT IS WHY WE ARE HERE.
TO SHOW LOVE. TO BE LOVE.
TO REFLECT LOVE."

-ANDREW

CHAPTER 3

By September, I was in a state of high anxiety, waiting. Monitoring was weekly, with the scheduled date for induction fast approaching. We had lined up Stuart's parents to take Andrew while we were in the hospital. Andrew would stay with them at their home, where he had stayed many times before. We had a plan. We were prepared.

At the same time, my close friend, Jade, was dying. Jade had been diagnosed with breast cancer. She embarked on a holistic healing journey that included only natural therapies and treatments, and although she extended her conventional medical prognosis by many months, in her words, her time had come. My last conversation with Jade was on a walk through the ravine behind her home. I could see it in her eyes; she knew she was dying. It wasn't that she had given up; she had surrendered—a task most of us struggle to master over far lesser tribulations and with far less grace. She was ready to let go. What I loved about Jade was the balance she maintained between her deep spiritual existence and her down-to-earth presence. She was real in every sense of the word. We laughed hard and cried even harder together. She was a true soul sister, a dear friend.

The day she told me she was dying I knew would be the last time I would see her.

Two days before my scheduled induction, I got a call that Jade had died. The news took my breath away. I finally broke down; all the optimism and stamina I had mustered to endure the months of my own fragility vanished. Lying in bed, my pregnant body shook with sobs, my tears soaking my pillow until there were none left.

I would not thoroughly grieve the loss of this close friend until many years later. I would not be able to attend her funeral, nor could I support her grieving husband or the children Jade left behind. I would be consumed by my own son's delicate medical state, far beyond anything I could have anticipated.

On September 23, 2010, we woke up early, bags already packed. Andrew was settled at my in-laws. We expected we might need a few extra days in the hospital, not knowing what complications may present and where they would take us. Stuart's parents were happy to have Andrew stay with them indefinitely.

We arrived at Mount Sinai Hospital at the suggested time. We were excited and anxious, ready to finally meet this little person and learn how to best support him. We waited hours to be seen, perplexed by what was taking so long, adding to our state of anxiety. I listened to music through headphones, a few meaningful, comforting songs on repeat, but even that got stale. Finally, late afternoon, we were admitted. We settled into a standard labor and delivery room. We got out our snacks and set up music. I began walking around to help move things along. There were no signs my body was ready to go into labor naturally, so our nurse made a tiny tear in my uterine sac with hopes it would induce labor. I continued to walk around with no change. Within an hour, we agreed to medically induce our labor.

As quick as my water broke and the Pitocin coursed through my veins, the contractions began. Fast and furious (not uncommon with a medically induced labor), they brought back a tidal wave of cellular memories: the harrowing time I'd had laboring with

Andrew—the intense pain, the feeling of being out of control, and the speed at which it was all happening. I remembered it vividly.

I looked at Stuart in desperation. I had coached him prior to this moment (which I knew would come) to never suggest an epidural, even if I begged him, even if he saw me in agony, even if the memory of Andrew's labor came rushing back to him too. Knowing and respecting my desire for a natural labor, he said nothing. But from a voice outside of myself, in a calm, steady, and familiar tone, I heard the words: "Get the f*cking epidural."

It was Jade. She was with me.

There was no mistaking that down-to-earth voice of hers. And those words were something she would say. She was giving me permission.

With tears in my eyes, I laughed out loud and announced I wanted an epidural. Stuart was surprised but supportive. We lined it all up. It was bliss. I stretched out, flipping through magazines on my belly and eating chips while my contractions moved along. We shook our heads at the complexity of it all.

Jade knew something I didn't.

I would need my strength. If I could spare myself from the exhaustion of anything near what I experienced in Andrew's labor, I would be more prepared for the hours and days ahead, though nothing could truly prepare me for what was to come.

***

It was time. The nurses transferred us, wheeling my bed to a nearby delivery room directly beside the neonatal emergency room. They anticipated our baby needing immediate medical assistance upon birth. I was fully dilated and ready to deliver.

After three easy pushes, a mere ten-minute delivery, James was born. He was placed in my arms. I was overjoyed to see him; he was finally here. He let out a cry, but his cry wasn't normal—it was stifled and not what we expected. The doctor mumbled something I couldn't hear, then whisked James away to the neonatal emergency room. I caught only a glimpse of his beautiful face and felt only a fleeting moment of the weight of his seven-pound perfect body in my arms.

He was unable to breathe; the X-rays showed that not only had his kidney not developed properly but his lung capacity hadn't either. His lungs were a healthy size, but their surface area for breathing was underdeveloped (a potential result of low amniotic fluid levels very early on in pregnancy and something you can't see in utero). He was intubated, put on a respirator, and heavily examined in a room I couldn't see, in a place I couldn't access.

In our tiny post-delivery room, we waited. Quickly forgotten, my physical experience of labor and delivery was replaced by the acute reality that we were without our newborn son. Sitting together on the edge of the hospital bed, Stuart and I tried to recount what had just happened:

Did they tell us where James will be? How long they will take? Or when we'll be able to see him again?

We waited hours for an update.

At some point a doctor came in to see us. It was all so clinical. No cordialities. No cards and flowers. Instead, it was medical reports and updates.

It was confirmed that James's underdeveloped kidney was not functioning adequately, though he was able to produce urine. What was more concerning, however, was James's lung capacity that impacted his ability to breathe, to exchange carbon dioxide for oxygen, to sustain life itself. He would remain on life support while the medical team continued their examinations. They brought us in to see him. There he was, our beautiful baby boy, full and alive, lying on an incubator bed with tubes and IVs draped across his little body.

James had been taken out of my arms as quickly as he'd been placed there. And now here he was before me, helpless (both of us). Me, unable to hold him, to protect him, to breathe life into him. Nine months of carrying him, feeding him, and nurturing him. Now, nothing I could do to help him.

I remember feeling like time stood still within those stark hospital walls, like the rest of the world carried on while we spent long hours waiting, praying, wondering. It was all so traumatic and surreal.

"Baby" was all it said on his clear plastic incubator until we gave him the name James. He was always James, stoic and noble, it just became clearer to us as his strength presented in those first twenty-four hours of his life.

James lived in the neonatal intensive care unit (NICU). And for seven days, so did we. He was born at Mount Sinai, but when his case required the best in the field of neonatal intensive care, he was transferred to Toronto's Hospital for Sick Children (SickKids), right across the street. He was whisked through an underground tunnel, from Mount Sinai to SickKids, under Toronto's busy University Avenue. In the dead of night, cars and taxis and buses above would never know that a newborn baby, tethered by tubes to beeping monitors, IVs, and ventilators just a few meters below, was fighting for his life.

Still in the postnatal delivery ward, I sobbed while staring out the window into the night, sick that my baby boy had to travel by himself through that cold, hollow passage without his parents, without a warm hand or a familiar voice to carry him to safety. What a brave, strong soul he was. I could be that brave too.

Once we heard that James had been stabilized, we tried to sleep—me still in a postnatal recovery bed, and Stuart uncomfortably bent across a visitor's chair at my side—but with no success. As the sun rose, with my request to be discharged, we carried our small travel bags across University Avenue. We had preemptively packed emergency clothes and toiletries with the understanding that our high-risk baby might need to stay longer and that we might need to stay longer as well.

***

Arriving at SickKids felt surreal. *Is this really happening? Is this us? Where is James?* Staff escorted us to the third floor, the NICU, the place where the sickest babies in all the hospital stayed.

We saw it all: babies on ventilators, babies with their intestines outside of their abdomen, babies as small as your palm, all hooked up to tubes and wires and monitors. Our baby was one of those babies. Just days old, there he was, intubated and alone. We rushed to his bedside, the clear plastic walls of his NICU bed the only thing separating him from us. Except that he felt a world away, untouchable.

We carried tiny cotton cloths with us, tucked inside our shirt and against our skin, so that when they were placed by James's bedside, he could smell us. We pinned a tiny family photo of the three of us—Stuart, Andrew, and me—to the edge of his bed. I continued to pump any milk my breasts made with the hope that, at some point, maybe James could taste it. We sang to him, songs we could muster the words to, often church songs that came back to me. "You Are Near," "On Eagle's Wings," and "Be Not Afraid," I sang through my choked tears. We held on to the hope that he could hear us and smell us and see us, and that one day he would be with us again. In the meantime, this was how we connected.

We stayed by his side, pulling spare stools up to his bedside in the NICU. Hour after hour, nurses and doctors checked the monitors, assessing his vitals: his blood oxygen levels, blood sugar levels, urine output, and other markers. They were gentle and compassionate. They talked to James during their rounds, explaining what they were doing, or that they liked the picture of his family, or that he was doing well. They were also professional and quick to tell Stuart and me that we would need a longer-term plan: a room we could go to for reprieve and somewhere to sleep. Uncommonly done, but because our case was acutely fragile, NICU staff arranged a room for us down the hall. There was a foldout double bed, a private bathroom, a table, some chairs, and a little fridge. This would be our home for the next five days.

It all became a blur. Minutes felt like hours, hours felt like days. Stuart and I spent most of our time at James's side. Still, staff encouraged us to take walks, get fresh air outside, and eat. So we did. We were robotic yet completely lucid, present in every moment.

We accepted no visitors, save for our immediate family, all who came to James's bedside to meet him, including Stuart's sister who flew in from Australia. My longtime friend, the one who had introduced me to Stuart some ten years prior, also came to see us. People who had learned we were there came to the NICU, leaving cards and flowers at the reception desk. A few holistic nutrition friends dropped off food, desperate to do *something*, anything. Everyone helplessly offered words of comfort and sympathy, knowing there was nothing they could say that would truly ease our pain.

So preoccupied with James, we rarely thought about Andrew. We knew he was content with his grandparents. One of the days, at our request, Stuart's parents brought Andrew to the NICU to meet James. Stuart and I carried our two-year-old toddler into the busy quadrant of the NICU where James lived. Hoisted on my hip, I held my chubby, rosy boy up to the side of James's bed for him to see his baby brother.

I will never forget, through my tears, the joy I felt seeing Andrew gaze upon him. They knew each other, somehow, Andrew and James. On some level, I knew they would always know each other.

The visit was short; it was all Andrew could manage. We said goodbye and watched as Andrew happily strode off with Nana and Poppa. It was the last time Andrew would ever see James.

***

Some days were lighter than others. Some days Stuart and I laughed at the little things, like maybe something that had happened in our 12' x 12' hospital room. Some days we would feel optimistic about James's state, believing that things would turn around, hoping that one day we would all go home.

Some days were heavy. The dismal reality of our son's prognosis would stare us in the face through the blaring lights and sounds of his vital monitors. Certain moments would weigh heavier on Stuart, other moments, on me. We were there for each other, noting how one would carry the other. Stuart would often say through his tears, "I don't know how you're so strong, Susan." I didn't know either. Something allowed me to persevere. Some days, though, I would cry and cry and wonder when it would end.

I remember standing at the NICU reception desk with my dad on a day when my parents had visited. He had a simple way of framing things. Seeing me distraught, he said to me, "This will end." He wasn't being insensitive; he was right. In one way or another, it *would* end.

We had regular meetings with James's medical team in a tiny consult room just off the main NICU hallway. After countless tests, professional opinions, and examinations, it was determined that our precious baby boy had two major organ systems in failure: his lungs and his kidneys. There was nothing more they could do.

We couldn't fix our baby, not with all the medical experts and treatments in the world. We were faced with the reality that, for James to truly experience living, we had to set him free. We would have to remove the ties that were keeping him bound to his physical body, his physical life, so that his soul could truly live. It was one of the most excruciating decisions we would ever have to make.

And so, on his seventh day, we would set him free.

The nurses wheeled James in, still in his NICU bed, hooked up to life support. Most of the other tubes and IVs had already been removed, and he came to us without most of his monitors. He came into our room, our little home away from home, where we greeted him that one final day. A kind, familiar nurse had lifted James out of his delicate bed and placed him in my arms.

For the first time, he felt real. Sitting in that hospital chair, I could feel the weight of his body against mine. I could touch him and smell him, finally. Stuart smiled, holding James's hand, caressing his face.

James was beautiful. We told him how proud we were to be his parents; how proud we were of his courage and his strength; that, because of him, we had learned *our* strength. We told him we were grateful to have had that time with him; grateful to know him. We told him that we loved him.

He died in my arms. As Stuart stood beside me, holding my hand and one of James's, we wept. We wept for all of the days that led to this moment, and we wept for all of the days that would never be. We wept at the sheer loss of it all.

Holding him, I watched a veil come over James, then peace. Overcome by this, I could only assume that I had witnessed a soul's journey through death and passing on. It took my breath away. What was left was beauty and peace. One of the most spiritual experiences of my life, it was the closest to God I had ever felt. I felt no anger, amid my pain and agony, only love.

James was gone.

We shared a few moments, James, Stuart, and me, before the nurses pulled a blanket up over his head and lovingly took him from my arms. They carried him out of our room, wheeling his bed behind them.

We were alone again. We were numb.

What happened next I can only recall from a bird's-eye view, just like the day when I watched myself receive the news from the midwife of James's complications. I see myself, from above, sitting on the bed, my head in my open hands, weeping. My body trembling. Stuart beside me, holding me, grieving too. Then, moments later, a door opens and it's Andrew. He runs in. Eyes wide, joyful, he runs straight into my arms. He holds me; it's as though he knows. Of course he does. I hug him. "We can go home now," I say to him. I tell him how happy I am to see him. And I am, so happy. The rest of our family follows, my parents and Stuart's parents. They have been waiting to come in, waiting in the visitors' room, waiting to be told that it was time. No words were exchanged, just tears. Deep hugs holding the promise of support, of sympathy, and of love.

We gathered our belongings, our sorrow and our grief, and walked out through the hospital doors. We left with an empty car seat.

"MAY WE NEVER UNDERESTIMATE
THE IMPACT OUR STORY HAS
ON ANOTHER."
-SUSAN

CHAPTER 4

Life changed for me the day James died. My experience of motherhood changed. The path that led before me moved in a direction I hadn't expected. One I could never have predicted.

We were in shock and disbelief, our minds busy, trying to process all of what had come. Life wasn't supposed to go this way; babies weren't supposed to die. Babies, stillbirths, miscarriages, even the loss of a child who could never be conceived—none of it.

Becoming a mother, you learn it's all about love. Sometimes you don't get to choose when you love, how hard you love, or how deep. And sometimes the love you feel actually hurts. Sometimes great love ends in great loss.

I remember, just days after arriving home, standing in the shower and weeping as I watched milk stream from my breasts. I cried, heaved, then laughed in delirium at the trauma of it all.

How can this be? How can I be home without my baby? How could this happen?

I could hardly label it, hardly make sense of it; it was all just so excruciatingly sad. So I stopped trying. It was beyond me. After all, it was a journey not of the mind but of the soul.

There is such tragedy, pain, and loss in this life. We lose our parents, our friends, a partner. A sister, a brother, our child. Nothing ever takes away that loss; it becomes part of who we are.

We can't control what life brings; we can't control what we are meant to endure or who we are meant to become. For me, this is where faith lies. My spiritual beliefs allowed me to endure the pain of this experience, to persevere, and to trust in the process of life, even if it didn't make sense. I should have lost all faith, and yet I felt carried that week with James; I felt held. Faith was all I had.

Perhaps knowing that James had complications was, in fact, a gift. Knowing he was at risk of failure meant we were prepared to meet his needs upon birth. It gave us one week with him, one week where Stuart and I learned our strength and our weaknesses. Would I have traded this? Wished the pain away? Wished it had never happened in the first place? Not ever. It was a gift to be able to tell James we loved him. It was a gift to be able to say goodbye. We would have never known James, and James was a gift to us all.

Unbeknownst to us, his story of struggle and hope traveled beyond the hospital walls that week. He inspired hundreds of people—from solitary prayers and positive thoughts to email chains and healing circles—across our community and beyond. We received countless cards and messages and words of support and sympathy, but also stories of how James's life had renewed a spiritual strength in them, or fostered their own personal growth, even when the outcome was what it was.

That one week brought Stuart and me closer together than we'd ever been before. We rebuilt our foundation as a couple. We grew in love and strength and vulnerability.

James's life was not lost.

I ordered all of James's medical records and never read them. I'm not sure I ever will.

***

No one knew what to say. Encountering neighbors, people I had walked by for nine months who had watched my belly grow, who grew in excitement along with me, were speechless. Seeing their faces fall, their awkwardness as I approached with no baby by my side—managing *their* reaction, their discomfort, overshadowed managing my own.

Stuart and I found ourselves consoling others. It was a relief when someone would apologetically mumble, "I don't know what to say," because they were right; there were no words. Instead, sympathy came through dropped-off casseroles and homemade meals. Our neighbors and friends were grieving along with us. None of us knew how to do it except to just allow for all of it.

To find closure, we held a funeral at our local Catholic church. It's what I knew. I thought it might help Stuart and me mark the end of this chapter of our life. Hundreds flooded the church. Family and friends, people from all different circles, came out to show their sorrow and deep caring. Fellow nutritionists, work colleagues, neighbors, cycling friends of Stu's, old family friends, camp friends, high school friends, our parents' friends—the pews filled. Something about James's life had touched others. We were all searching for something to help make sense of this tragedy. I'm not sure any of us found it within the walls of that church, but there was a coming together that day, a closure and a peace around the story of James.

Stuart and I stood on the altar and delivered the eulogy we had prepared. We read with composure, no one quite sure how we had the strength to speak the words. Perhaps we were numb. In truth, it's what we believed: that James's life was a gift and that it was meant to be as it was. It had taught us hope, humility, and surrender. Life was about something much bigger than us, we learned.

It was a beautiful time and a tragic time in our life. Stuart and I felt close, yet separated by our grief.

Stuart grieved differently than I. (I worried he didn't grieve at all.) Trusting that we were both on our own healing path, I watched as Stuart processed his grief in quiet ways. Cycling was his solace. Perhaps a lot can be worked through on a bike.

Then one day Stuart came home beaming. He told me about a little curly-haired redhead who bounced into his life on the subway ride home from work. "Hi! My name's Abby!" she had announced to him. She was only about three years old, he guessed. She proceeded to tell him all about her life while her mother smiled on, knowingly and patiently. She had lit up Stuart's day. I hadn't seen him this joyful, this hopeful, in a while.

"If we are fortunate enough to have another child one day, we will name her Abby, and she will be pure joy," he said with tears in his eyes. For Stuart, this little girl on the subway represented hope. Abigail, translated from its original Hebrew origin, means "father's joy."

There would be joy again.

One cool gray day I took Andrew out for a walk, the very same walk we had done countless times before. Something felt different. As we rounded the bend from the street into the ravine, there stood in front of us, almost mystical, a tree. A new tree, an oak. A tiny, strong oak sapling had been planted in James's memory, for us. Our neighbors, the same ones who delighted in our pregnancy and mourned our loss, had come together to honor our family.

We called it "James's tree," a tree we would pass time and time again and could visit to remind us of the time we had spent with our sweet baby boy. A beautiful oak tree, delicate yet strong and full of purpose, just like James.

"LOVE ABOVE ALL THINGS."

–ANDREW

CHAPTER 5

It was all a lot. Losing James was monumental for our family. It took us weeks to find ourselves again, to regroup and recollect what life was like "before James." Weeks turned into months, and although there was extreme stress, tension, and sadness in our home, the pain lessened.

We were surrounded by a community of people who cared very much—friends, family, neighbors. They checked in on us, but I still felt alone. Life felt lonely. I wanted to feel happy again, to feel like myself again. I never wanted to admit I was sad or worried about Andrew. Friends would call, family would drop in, but those solitary days, just Andrew and me, felt long and empty.

We wondered if Andrew had regressed during this time. So much energy had gone into James's pregnancy and birth, we weren't surprised that we were seeing more peculiarities in Andrew. We felt worried and frustrated by his development.

As his mother, I loved our time together, but it required effort to engage with Andrew. He seemed very much in his own world—content, but to himself. For a while I thought that it was okay; we were similar, in that way. I loved being on my own, spending time by myself. But I would watch other moms with their toddlers and see an automatic, natural interaction. We had that too, but ours was more of an unspoken connection. A deeper knowing.

We would stand at the river, a place Andrew loved, just listening to the rippling water. He would tilt his head to one side, adjusting it ever so slightly so as to position his ear in just the right place, and smile. He would look up at the sky, at the treetops, at the fluttering leaves, and grin. We would be there for hours.

I started going to the mom-and-tot group less. With no new baby in tow (a baby the group had expected to be along with me), plus a toddler who didn't play like the others, I was no longer a typical parent. I wondered, Was I harder to talk to? Did people not know what to say to me? These were women I had gotten to know in the neighborhood. I felt I could no longer relate. It became more and more obvious to all of us that my little boy who had babbled alongside their toddlers was headed down a different path. He wouldn't play cars (except to throw them) and he didn't play house (except to "listen" to plastic toy food at his ear). It became too much for me to bear.

People have always asked, "When did you know Andrew was autistic?" It was then. I just didn't want to face it. I couldn't; I was exhausted. Depleted from the weeks and months of carrying the complex life of James in my heart, I couldn't bear the thought that Andrew might also have challenges. But I could no longer turn away. It was staring right at me: my child was definitely *different*.

One particular day just weeks after having lost James, I dropped Andrew off at a morning playgroup for toddlers in our local community center. I wanted life to feel normal. I figured developing a new routine would help. I needed to learn how to live as a mother to just Andrew again. And I needed to bring myself back to me.

I could never remember where that time went or what I did. I just know I needed it. I was numb. Part of me grieving was remembering how to operate in day-to-day life. I still needed to grocery shop and make meals, to answer emails and prepare for my part-time work contracts. (I had said yes to work to keep my mind occupied once I knew I would not be home with a newborn.)

But I would find myself just staring—staring into an open fridge, staring at the laundry, staring at my phone. Not much got done in those free mornings.

When I went to pick up Andrew that one particular day, I was paralyzed by the reality of his development. I observed him sitting by himself in front of a box of toy cars, throwing them one by one across the room. Normally I would smile and say something whimsical like "Well *that's* a new way of playing with cars!" But not this time. This time, I couldn't ignore it. I could no longer hold myself up with the positive perspective of how easily Andrew could amuse himself with the simplest of things, of how unique and creative he was. I saw things differently that day. My heart raced; my breath quickened. I felt panicked, worried, and sad. Something was not right.

"He's been doing that most of the morning, just throwing things across the room. He doesn't play much with the other kids, does he? And does he talk? Because he hasn't been talking with us. Just keeping to himself. Have you taken him to his doctor yet, because you probably should look into it . . . "

I was angry, tears in my eyes. I grabbed Andrew, poignantly said something to staff about embracing individuality, and whisked him away.

We sat in the car in the parking lot, me in the front seat and Andrew behind me in his car seat, and I yelled. "Why are you like this? Why can't you play normally like the other children? What is wrong with you?" I yelled at him and I yelled at God. "What the hell! Haven't I had enough? Can't you let up for a second?" And then I sobbed. I sobbed for the loss of James, in frustration for Andrew, and in heart-wrenching pity for myself.

And then I called his pediatrician.

***

It was the first time I ever admitted that something might not be right with my child–that it might be worth looking at, worth better understanding, worth getting help.

The pediatrician's office scheduled a visit for us just weeks later. I remember it vividly: sitting there, waiting for the doctor to come into the little treatment room, watching Andrew spin cups on the floor, my heart beating through my chest, choking back tears. It was all coming to a head.

"Hi, Susan. Hi, Andrew. How are things?" And so it began. I explained to the doctor why we were there. That I had recently observed Andrew acting and playing *differently*. That his speech was delayed. (He was almost two and a half and was still only using word approximations, and very few at that. "Dah" for Dad, "puh-puh" for purple, "nah ha" for not hot–but even those were few and far between.) I figured we should know if something was going on, something we needed to be aware of, in order to help Andrew. Truthfully, though, I was hoping the doctor wouldn't see it.

I even jokingly said, "I expect you'll say to me: 'Oh, Susan, you're a grieving mother. You're being hypervigilant about Andrew, worried, and seeing things bigger than they are. Why don't you go home and put your feet up . . . '"

But he didn't say that.

Instead, he got out developmental checklists and red-flagged us for autism. "Delayed language development . . . limited or no interest in other children . . . playing with toys in an unusual manner . . . " He listed off sign after sign. It was like hearing someone describe my child from a book, yet all of what I was hearing were aspects of Andrew I held as unique. The traits that, I thought, made him who he was.

The writing was on the wall.

It was the beginning of what would end up being months and years of terms like "early intervention," "atypical," and "delayed."

I left the pediatrician's office feeling like someone had punched me in the stomach. My mind was dizzy. I was exhausted, emotionally and physically, like I had run a race. It was a race that was only just beginning. In fact, it would be a marathon.

After that initial visit, Stuart went into research mode, looking up signs of autism, therapies to help with communication, and what life might look like for a family that had a disability. I did not. Part of me didn't believe it was autism, or what I knew to be autism. I wanted to believe that this was just who my child was: a unique, whole individual.

The pediatrician explained the process to us. We would be contacted by our region's Early Intervention Services to set up home visits for strategies for what we could do while we waited for an actual assessment with the children's treatment network.

We were on a path to a diagnosis. I knew it, though I had no idea what that meant.

I would hear myself making sense of it all. Words would come, words I could recite as an explanation for who my child was, for his behavior, his noises, for what he was doing (or wasn't doing). Justifications and apologies.

Inevitably, someone *would* require an explanation.

Like on one of our beloved walks, there was the perplexed woman who stopped to look at Andrew standing, head titled, with a pine cone at his ear. She said, "Oh, I'm so sorry" when I explained to her that it might be autism.

Or at the library drop-in for story time, where we lasted only ten minutes, when Andrew wailed, hands covering his ears, and the lovely librarian (really, she was) said, "Don't worry about us, just worry about your child" while the other parents just stared, probably in empathy. I wanted to grab him and squeeze him hard and say "Shut up! Just, shut up!" wishing Andrew would love the library program like all the other kids.

Or the dad at the park who swung his child in the swing next to ours, who didn't know what to say at the sound of Andrew's noises and squeals of delight, so he didn't say anything.

Or at the coffee shop, which was an outing and a break for me, which ended with Andrew throwing his snack and biting his wrist, unexplained, and I had to say to the older man who was staring at us that Andrew was overwhelmed and maybe it was because he was autistic but we didn't know yet, and the man briskly responded with "Shame. Well, I hope you find a way to fix it."

Truth is, in my mind, they were only half wrong. Part of me did feel sorry for us. Part of me did want Andrew to be like all the other kids. Part of me did want to "fix" him.

Surely all the tools I had as a holistic health practitioner, all the books I had read and the speakers I had heard, would help me heal my child so that it didn't look like autism anymore.

I had learned about children who had "recovered." Children who had dropped their diagnosis, or their diagnoses, after various treatments and therapies. Wouldn't I want that to be *my* child? Wasn't that the goal? Or was it?

I didn't see my child as a "puzzle." I never connected with the symbolism of blue hearts for autism or multicolored puzzle pieces. I resisted functioning labels and levels of ability. My child was his own person. I didn't need an autism campaign or a charity to represent him.

But I felt sad. I brought this beautiful child into the world and I didn't know how to reach him. Finally seeing that he was, in fact, developing *differently*, and maybe in a way that I didn't fully understand, I wanted to take that which didn't feel "okay" and make it into something that did. But I didn't know how.

Those days were hard. Stuart and I argued a lot. Some days the tension could be cut with a knife. We were both still grieving and trying to make sense of the child in front of us. We sought counseling and marital support. We both just wanted to feel like ourselves again.

In time, things softened. We were learning how to parent a child who was "different," and although there was stress, we were finding our way. Stuart and I had built a solid foundation. We loved each other. We were able to laugh and live in the fun of our true personalities again. We would put music on, make jokes, and enjoy each other's company.

Growing our family was never far from our hearts. Losing James affirmed what Stuart and I both knew: we wanted another child, a sibling for Andrew, an expansion of our family's love.

I desired so badly to be pregnant, though a close friend, an obstetrician, pleaded with me to wait, to give my body time to heal. It was something I could not control. Yet again, I would need to let go and trust.

Then, as winter turned to spring, with the promise of rebirth, we were pregnant. We were pregnant! What a myriad of emotions:

relief, joy, worry, hesitation, concern, elation, warmth, and love. Not surprising after what we'd been through.

So now what? Do we need to see a doctor? When will we tell our family?

And then, of course, there was the looming question: *Will everything be okay?*

The vivid pain of our loss came rushing back. Ecstatic as I was to be pregnant, I cried thinking of James. Were we replacing him? Could we love this new child for who they were, not as a substitute for James or a shadow of what should have been?

More than anything, we were excited. We were moving forward.

"COURAGE IS SHOWING UP,
EVEN WHEN IT'S HARD TO."
-ANDREW

CHAPTER 6

I have emails that date back to this exact period of our life. Emails with sonogram images announcing our healthy pregnancy. I have reread them in awe, marveling at how courageous we were to move through fear and pain into trust and hope.

I was pregnant again and we were thrilled. Having it confirmed by blood work and a first-trimester ultrasound brought great relief to Stuart and me. We told our family. Of course, they were elated. It was a mix of joy and trepidation for them too. We decided against genetic testing—not that we wanted to endure what we had with James, but knowing how rare his circumstances were, we trusted the natural process of this pregnancy to be healthy.

We chose to be in the care of a medical doctor at our local hospital, *just in case*. Our emotions were still fragile from the complexity of James's life and death. Our doctor knew our vulnerability and was sensitive to our needs. We would await the second-trimester anatomical scan to truly put our minds, and our hearts, at ease.

Of course, we excitedly shared the news with Andrew. What he understood of it, we weren't sure; he didn't pay much notice. We couldn't ask him if he was excited or if he thought it was a boy or a girl; he still wasn't speaking. Though there was love, he seemed to exist in his own world. He would show affection by sitting on my lap (nestled right next to my belly) or smelling my hair. He was soon to be three, a busy toddler, and though there were challenges, we had something new to focus on: our baby to be.

The day we went in for the second-trimester ultrasound, my anxiety peaked. Walking through the labor and delivery wing of the hospital for the first time since James had been born and seeing parents with their new babies brought in a flood of emotions. We'd never had that with James: being able to hold, or stay with, or carry home a new baby. I let myself feel it all.

Our results were normal. Our doctor lovingly, gently, shared that there were no signs of any anatomical or developmental abnormality as far as the ultrasound could show. We were going to have a healthy baby girl. We let out a huge sigh of relief, laughed, and then bawled. Our baby was due New Year's Eve. What a perfect new beginning.

It was summer. We were loving being outside more, Stuart was riding his bike again, and we could entertain Andrew by going for walks or listening to the babbling brook near our home. We even booked a trip to Paris for Stuart and me. I would be six months pregnant, mobile enough to tour around and not far along enough to worry about the end.

We fully enjoyed that time together in Paris. We felt carefree, vibrant, and alive. Andrew stayed with Stuart's parents who were more than capable, even with Andrew's increasing behavioral challenges and sensory needs. It was the break we needed. We could finally reflect on all we had been through and where we were headed. There was laughter and freedom again.

I found myself excited at the reality of being pregnant. I enjoyed watching my body change and seeing my belly grow, knowing there was a healthy developing life inside of me. I thought of James often and thanked him for his life. Albeit short, his life had purpose. Because of his life, there was a new life forming—one that would not replace his, but that could exist *because of* his.

Meanwhile, we had begun "early intervention" for Andrew. Intervention, I presumed, of what would otherwise be a dismal trajectory for a child with a "neurological disorder," according to the experts.

An enthusiastic pediatric therapist came to our home twice a week through public health. She excitedly sought Andrew's attention through various light-up toys, noisemakers, and her own melodic, juvenile intonations. I found them grating and condescending; I wondered what Andrew thought. He was somewhat amused. She worked hard to engage with him, modeling turn-taking through floor-time activities and imitation in our play kitchen. He didn't really seem to care. It felt hopeful and insulting: *Is this necessary? Teaching my child how to develop? Teaching my child how to be like everyone else?* I wasn't convinced, but like most concerned parents with an impending diagnosis and no sense of alternatives, we obliged.

Stuart and I attended a weekly communication course, called More Than Words, designed for parents of children with significant speech delays. We learned how to create "joint attention" with our child, physically getting down to his level, repeating what he did or vocalized, in an effort to show him that we were there *with him*, "in his world," and, I suppose, how good that could feel for him. Maybe for us too. It all felt very contrived.

It was a busy time. Although the medical appointments for my pregnancy had tapered off (all tests and measures showed a healthy, viable pregnancy), our commitment to Andrew was increasing. We were receiving guidance on how to engage with our son, which needed to be implemented. We would need to practice all of what we were learning. It took time, effort, and considerable patience.

Andrew was three and officially a busy toddler. His tantrums and demands were exacerbated by the fact that he had no means to express himself. He had no words, just a series of vocalizations, grunts, and screams to have his needs met. We were on a waitlist for a developmental assessment early the following year through our regional health unit, just months after our new baby would be born. We were grateful to our pediatrician for guiding us early on in this process.

Thankfully, we had much support. All four grandparents, each in their sixties, were actively involved in this stage of our family's life. We had found Andrew a home daycare that focused on the natural rhythm of a child's day, healthy whole foods, and being outside. It was Waldorf-based and very much aligned with our values around health and the importance, especially for Andrew, of being in nature. Andrew's grandparents would take turns driving Andrew so that I could teach (I had kept my foot in the door) or attend an appointment. Sometimes they watched Andrew at night, or had him sleep over, so that Stuart and I could attend a workshop or spend quality time together as a couple.

Still a go-getter, I had stayed connected to most aspects of my nutrition career. I loved what I did and it kept me alive: seeing clients, delivering health seminars, and teaching at the nutrition college. I worked whenever I could. Eventually, it would be reduced to very little, between Andrew's needs, therapies, and a new baby. I slowly began to wind down some of my commitments. Life was introducing new priorities. Having loved everything I was involved in, this was very hard for me to do. I had been raised to believe I was capable, smart, and could achieve anything I set my mind to, which I always expected meant a career *and* a family. But I had also been raised to know that being a parent at home was of value. Suddenly I felt the pressure of trying to have it all. Could I have it all?

I tried.

For me, "doing it all" meant that I wasn't doing it all *well*. Something had to give. For a while I resisted. Even in later years I resented the duty and responsibility I felt of being a mother. Letting go felt like loss, an unsolicited giving up of the things I loved. But when I truly slowed down to listen (something I wasn't accustomed to doing), I could hear a call to follow this path. Yes, a very other-centered life, but it would become a highly enriching and meaningful path for me.

More than a year passed between losing James and meeting our new baby. It had felt like an eternity, yet only a brief moment in time. We were ready. We had processed through the anxious anticipation of meeting this new life, the worry that we could not endure again what we had with James, and the fear that something might go wrong. We had learned to trust again.

One day in the weeks approaching our due date, I broke out into tears. Trembling, I heard myself whisper, "Please let me keep this one." I couldn't bear the thought of losing again.

I would trust and let go of what was beyond my control, all over again.

I knew there was joy ahead.

***

New Year's Eve came and went with no baby. We were officially overdue. A twinge of worry crept in as the days passed. Was something wrong? A follow-up ultrasound, just to be sure, confirmed everything was fine. Baby was cozy. Perhaps it was that I wasn't ready to let go.

On day ten, we were admitted to the hospital. Due to our increased anxiety based on our experience with James, we agreed to stimulate labor. I took a deep breath, reminding myself that I could do this. It was time to trust and let go. Within an hour I was in full, active labor. Only hours after that, our baby was born.

A gorgeous baby girl, pink and full of life, there she was, resting on my chest. Our labor and delivery had been healthy and routine. As she burst into our lives with vigor and determination, I laughed, then cried out to Stuart, "But can she breathe?"

Stuart, tears streaming down his face, exclaimed, "Yes, she can breathe."

Holding her, feeling her warm skin on mine, her chest rising and falling, I sobbed. There was joy again.

Stuart quickly announced her name: Abigail Joy, just like he vowed it would be. She was absolutely her father's joy. I had never seen Stuart so taken by another human being. He was in awe of this little creation, finding laughter in her movements and love in her face. Theirs would be a playful connection, a deep love for years to come.

My recovery was swift, for which I was grateful. I needed to keep up with the new dynamic, a toddler and a newborn, in our household. Abby was a joy, though we were conscious of the impact she would have on Andrew. Her cries, her noises, even just her presence became sources of stress for him. Always having been acutely sensitive to sound, his tolerance for Abby was minimal.

Those early days were long and memorable, some of which I wish I could forget. Within a few weeks we realized how disrupted life had become. In an effort to shield Andrew from the shrill cries of a newborn, I slept with Abby in our half-finished basement. Stuart and I felt like ships in the night, passing each other in the hallway or up and down the stairs. At one point in our delirium, we laughed outright: *What the heck has happened to our life? Who are we? Didn't we used to have fun?* Not anymore. This did not feel like living. This felt like chaos.

Most days of the week I would drive Andrew thirty minutes from our home to the home daycare he had attended for more than six months. It was like a second home, and I was thankful to have it—to be able to leave him somewhere I could trust, for his benefit and mine. He was cared for, accepted, and content. Our car rides, however, were excruciating. Abby hated being in her car seat and would scream from the moment we pulled out of the driveway to when we arrived. Andrew, who had no sensory or emotional tolerance for her tears, would cry in response.

I have vivid memories of looking in the rearview mirror and seeing faces wet with tears. I can feel the stress and tightness in my body, my racing heart, like a cellular memory from that time. It became so unbearable that I enlisted help. Stuart's mother, who lived only five minutes from us, would drive Andrew to his daycare. I would stay home with Abby. Other times, my parents, who were thirty minutes south of us in Toronto, would come up to be with Abby and I would take Andrew. Or I would have neighbors stay with Abby, or drive Andrew. I said yes to all options.

When we were home together, I found myself juggling Andrew's need for attention and comfort with the needs of a newborn: nursing, changing, rocking. Andrew, too, wanted to be rocked. He needed to be consoled. So did Abby. They both needed me and I couldn't do it all. I continuously felt my body, my nervous system, racked by sheer exhaustion.

I would watch Andrew throw soil from the plants in our home, crying, so completely overwhelmed by his sensory world and the sounds of a newborn baby. I would turn my head for a second, Abby tucked in the bouncy chair near my feet, only to whip back around at the piercing sound of her cries, her brother having bitten her hand, her arm, her foot.

I would watch Andrew draw blood from his own arm, biting or scratching it so frequently that it was raw; he was so beside himself, unable to manage life in his world.

I watched as Andrew regressed, having accidents in beds, on the floor, and outside. Everywhere.

Abby was up in the night, as most newborns are, but so was Andrew. Abby would cry, and in a desperate attempt to keep Andrew asleep, I would rush to her side and nurse her to keep her quiet. She became conditioned, eventually waking three to four times a night.

Andrew took hours to fall asleep. It was a daily ritual we dreaded: heading into bedtime, knowing we would need to sit with Andrew, right up against him (sometimes *on* him) to settle him to sleep. His body pulsated, unable to relax and release. The weight of our body and our warmth soothed him. Perhaps he couldn't let go of his day. Perhaps his sensory system was so overwhelmed, so saturated by the day's events—the sights, the sounds, the smells, the birds, the wind, the people—it couldn't let go.

We would alternate putting Andrew to bed. Some nights it would be so maddening that one of us would storm out of Andrew's room exasperated, yelling: "I can't do this! I'm going to kill him!" Words you would never admit to anyone. We would spell each other off; we had to, to survive.

Once Andrew was asleep, Stuart would isolate himself in our bedroom, hoping to get a decent night of rest so as to function at work the next day. Then I was on. I would pray for an easy night. Maybe Abby would only be up once. Maybe Andrew would sleep through. But that was never the case.

One morning, after a particularly difficult night with Abby who was up multiple times, and Andrew, waking just after midnight and then not falling back to sleep till the early hours of morning, I declared, exhausted, that something had to give.

I decided to "sleep train" Abby. I knew she was a textbook baby and would take to it right away—she just needed the structure. So we sent Andrew off to my in-laws for three nights, and by the morning of day four, Abby was sleeping through the night. Just like that. It helped, but it didn't change that Andrew was still up for hours every night.

Andrew would wake, start chirping (we called it), or fall into fits of uncontrollable laughter made worse by any scolding from us. We would beg him to stay in his bed, to go back to sleep. We would sing to him. We would practice deep breathing, hoping our calming presence would help calm him. Sometimes we would have to pin him to his bed, him lying on his stomach, to help him settle, to force his body to stop moving. He would writhe and squirm, resisting our hold, then eventually, his body would surrender. His breathing would deepen and he would fall back to sleep. We would celebrate the gain of another hour or two of sleep until Abby woke at the break of dawn. It was unbearable.

I cried a lot. Beyond sleep deprived, I was empty. One particular afternoon, exhausted from lack of sleep and just so frustrated with Andrew, I threw a blue plastic recycling bin down the hall toward him. Andrew just laughed hysterically, the kind of laughter that is maddening, rooted in sensory overload, not the kind that breaks the ice between an upset parent and their toddler. Between the crash of the bin and Andrew's laughter, we woke Abby. It was all becoming far too much to handle.

I sought social services. I needed someone to talk to about how I was coping, someone who would understand this type of family dynamic. Apparently, it's quite common for young families dealing with autism to experience extreme physical and emotional stress.

I never did tell anyone that my honest disclosure to that community social worker resulted in a letter and a visit from Children's Aid.

I didn't tell many people that I had to call my neighbor in desperation, afraid of my rage, worried I would either lose it or just crumble to the floor and give up.

I was "fine"; I was managing. Nothing was bad enough to truly worry about, but I was a shell of myself. We weren't thriving, that was certain.

Eventually, we hired a part-time helper, a woman in her fifties, who could do the day-to-day tasks like laundry and dishes. She stayed with Abby while I picked Andrew up at the end of his day. She went for walks with Andrew in the afternoons, after he was home, so I could make dinner. She helped me keep Andrew and Abby in separate rooms on days when Abby's busyness was too much for Andrew to manage. I envisioned developing a relationship with this woman, like a grandmotherly figure in the house, adding warmth and nurturing and care. But it wasn't so; there wasn't space for that. We were all just surviving.

This is the autism you see, the autism most people know. The explosions, the projectiles, the meltdowns. What you don't see is how hard the autistic person is working to hold it together, how hard that family is working to keep afloat. (If this was autism—we hadn't been diagnosed yet.) Not to be melodramatic, as I would give anything to tell a lesser story. It's just the truth.

Life felt unreal. I wanted to love life, to find joy in this life. I wanted to feel like myself again. I wanted to wake up and know that I could handle it, but I began each day with dread, hating being a mom. Yes, we were having fun with Abby, and there were times when we would marvel at how far we had come, the four (the five) of us. But life felt hard.

Then, on the morning of April 19, 2012, the waves came crashing in.

"WE ARE ALL BRAVER THAN WE GIVE OURSELVES CREDIT FOR."

−ANDREW

CHAPTER 7

Dear family,

We know Andrew is "totally in there," brilliant, sensitive, loving, and with a sense of humor. He has skills and behaviors that other children (typical or atypical) don't have. When we're feeling strong as parents (you know, when we've had a decent sleep, or the financial markets are okay, or when the sun is out), we know we can handle it. On our weak days, life feels a bit overwhelming. We love and accept Andrew for who he is in that moment, that day. When we're tired or stressed, we feel more vulnerable as Andrew's parents, and so that same amazing kid with some of his atypical tendencies (like hand flapping on his mouth or constant flipping through his books or seeming more in his own world) triggers something in us that makes us less patient, less tolerant, and more worried. Sometimes it's hard to keep perspective. But also, we're allowed to have the worry and vulnerability. I realize that now. We expect that Andrew will receive a diagnosis of autism and instead of feeling a gut-wrenching "Oh God, now what?" we want to feel that we can handle it. That it's not about the label but about getting to know Andrew and the support he needs to thrive.

xo Susan

I found this note among a string of emails written to our family months prior to the day of our developmental assessment for autism. Looking back, I can see how hard we were trying to accept what was in front of us. I can see how life started to feel a little easier, if only in its predictability: life was challenging with a newborn and a toddler who was *different*, and that's just how it was. But nothing would take away the darkness we felt the day it was confirmed to be autism. The day Andrew received his diagnosis.

On a dismal, gray morning in April, within the nondescript walls of a children's treatment center near our home, Andrew received a diagnosis of severe autism spectrum disorder (ASD). The words hung in the air, then fell to the floor in that tiny room. Andrew, oblivious to any of it, carried on, lining up blocks and spinning cups–adding salt to a wound.

Stuart and I were stunned. It was what we had expected, but now, made official, we felt distraught, overwhelmed, and alone.

The diagnosis was given without any promise of hope for the future. We were provided with a few handouts and a short list of websites we could go to for more information on autism.

My whole world shook. I had lost a baby, grieved a baby, and now here I was, grieving the loss of another child–the loss of his childhood and the life I had imagined for him. I had a new baby in tow, and a child with significant needs. This had been the start of my motherhood.

I was angry, defensive, and, if I'm honest, probably in denial. Autism (or what I knew of autism) was not Andrew. But I didn't really know autism. What I knew of it was negative, difficult, and just plain sad. I didn't want this for Andrew or for us.

Stuart was quiet. Perhaps he felt relieved labeling what he saw in his son. If this was, in fact, *something*, then that meant we could do something about it. I remember feeling separate in our relationship, less unified than we had been through the loss of James. We both took the diagnosis to mean different things. I worried it would diminish who my child was, his uniqueness, his depth, and his individuality. Stuart merely saw it as confirmation of what we'd been observing, objective and action oriented.

Looking back, I can see why the possibility of Andrew having autism, even the word *autism* itself, triggered fear and resistance in me. *Autism* meant something was wrong, in my mind. These were the kids who tantrumed inconsolably, were unapproachable, who banged their head, who rocked back and forth, or who curled up in a ball. As a holistic nutritionist, my understanding had been that "children with autism" had reacted to vaccinations, ate poorly, were constipated, had recurrent infections and multiple rounds of antibiotics, or had too much screen time and never spent any time outside. Completely ignorant, I (clearly) knew very little about autism, and what I knew, wasn't Andrew. None of it was Andrew.

"Nonverbal," "low functioning," and "severe" were terms tossed around like news headlines. There was no light at the end of the tunnel, no perspective of what life *could be* like if we did X, Y, Z. No suggestions for therapies or health supports like diet or supplements, save for a few photocopied pieces of paper the doctor had given us upon receiving Andrew's diagnosis. Listed were standard autism therapies like Applied Behavior Analysis (ABA) and speech and language and, if the child exhibited self-injurious or dangerous behaviors, possibly antipsychotic medications down the road.

Andrew was still not talking, and there was no expectation for that to change. With very little guidance from the medical community, we began navigating the path on our own. We researched autism therapy centers in the community, tapped into parent resource groups, and continued attending the More Than Words communication course for parents of children who weren't yet speaking. There, we met a speech and language pathologist (SLP) who referred us to an autism center only fifteen minutes from our home. The clinical director of the center had worked with many children like Andrew and was the first to truly give us hope for the future, a life for Andrew that included self-sufficiency, independence, and the ability to communicate. Both the SLP and the clinical director would be involved in our family's life for years to come, even after we moved out of the area and into Toronto.

What perplexed me was that Andrew understood everything; he was clearly aware of what was going on around him, though it didn't always look that way. We could tell by the way he'd follow us to the door if we said we were leaving, or how he would respond warmly to his grandparents when they visited. It was all quite the opposite of the books we were reading that said autistic children were unemotional and unaware. Although he wouldn't always respond to his name, we knew he had heard us. (I even had his hearing checked to confirm there was no impairment.) He was listening. Perhaps he was taking it all in.

I truly believed that Andrew was not *wrong*, that his life was as meaningful as anyone's—mine, Abby's, James's. Deep within me I grew excited in the belief that children like Andrew were part of "an evolution of humanity," a new way of viewing the world. Andrew brought an awareness to what mattered: the importance of just *being*, feeling, experiencing life, finding and being in joy, and trusting our intuition.

Even in the hard, I never felt that Andrew's life shouldn't have existed. Still, the reality that my child was *different*, and that this could be hard, weighed on my heart. I would look at Andrew and know that he was *in there*. I believed that he was whole. I mean, who was telling me he wasn't? Doctors? School systems? Society?

I used to feel sad. Sad because I didn't know how to reach him or if anything would ever change. And yes, I *wanted it to change*. I wanted things to be easier. I did. I wanted to feel more connected. I wanted him to look at the birds with me, but instead, he'd be more interested in the blue sky and the trees in the foreground. I had come so far with acceptance, but *that one day*, I just wanted him to share in that moment. "Look, Andrew, look at the birds!" After many attempts, I had to let it go.

I have hated "the autism." I have cried and screamed and felt frustrated beyond words, kind of like Andrew. Can you imagine navigating your whole life—feeling hungry or needing a break or going to school for the first time—all without words? Without being able to ask a single question of your world?

Sometimes I've wished it wasn't my life, and sometimes I can't believe it *is* my life. It was not the life we had imagined. Me, Stuart, our two children, soccer practices and school festivals, happy Christmases, road trips, and travel. Special moments and words exchanged. Would there be any of that? Where was this going? How had we even gotten here?

Somehow, though, even when wishing it wasn't my life, I knew we could do this.

***

Abby was a lot of fun. Busy, explorative, creative, and resourceful—making up her own games, entertaining herself when I was not around. It's all she knew and she was happy. She was spirited and joyful. I would pray for the energy and enthusiasm to show up for her. It meant spending dedicated moments with Abby: an impromptu tea party on the kitchen floor; "baking cookies" in her play kitchen; or reading a book, with Andrew spinning cups in the background.

Abby loved life and that included her brother. Even when Andrew was distressed, she loved him regardless. My hope was that she wouldn't remember him taking it out on her, that the only lasting memory would be the scar on her cheek from the day he bit her in the grocery store parking lot, the day they were both screaming in the back seat of the car, the day I couldn't get to them fast enough to prevent it from happening. One of the many days I will never forget.

Abby adored Andrew. She watched him as he played and as he sat on the floor, flipping through his books and studying their pages—the brightly colored illustrations, the images, the words. Over and over, he would flip through them. A collection of well-read "Andrew books" sat in a basket in our family room.

In time, Andrew started showing affection toward Abby. I would catch him leaning over to smell the top of her head and feel her fine hair on his mouth. Sometimes he would look over at her and just watch her. Certainly, they were connected. I knew that, perhaps in a way I didn't fully understand. Maybe I didn't need to.

One day, the same as any other, we set out on our walk down the path we had taken so many times before. Andrew, running ahead. Abby, in a baby carrier on my chest. Me, stopped in front of James's tree.

I watched Andrew laughing at the wind, and as I kissed the top of Abby's soft head, it all just hit me. I wept. I cried for the loss of a child and the loss of a typical childhood for Andrew. I cried out of emotional exhaustion. Mostly, I cried tears at what struck me in that moment. There was Andrew, joyfully experiencing the beauty of life, the things we miss because we are too busy looking elsewhere. Then I thought of James's one week. Something profound occurred to me: Maybe we don't need to be fixed to truly experience living. Maybe life isn't a puzzle to be solved. Maybe it is all about allowing ourselves to truly live.

It was the first time I had felt at peace since becoming a mother.

That one week with James taught me my strength. It taught me a strength I didn't know I had, one that I would need in the years to come. It taught me I was resilient, but that it's okay to feel weak. It taught me to find joy, even amid pain. That one week with James showed me my courage, even in times of doubt and despair.

I stood there for a while, Abby bouncing under me, Andrew playing in the trees. I could do this; I could do this life. More than that, I knew then that this life was meant for me.

And so began my journey of supporting my child, not of fixing him. Of loving Abby for the person *she* was, not just as the sibling she would be to Andrew. And of recognizing our foundation as a couple, Stuart and me, and building our family's life on that.

I didn't know it then, but I see it now. I am a stronger person for both my children because of having had James.

"MAYBE WE DON'T NEED TO BE FIXED
TO TRULY EXPERIENCE LIVING."

-SUSAN

CHAPTER 8

By the summer of Andrew's fourth birthday, he was attending an autism center a few minutes from our home. Set in a bungalow-style house with large rooms and an outdoor play space with trees and a wide-open backyard, it felt ideal. The teaching philosophy was naturalistic; the directors were more interested in the children learning real-life constructs (for example: here's how a ball can be touched, rolled, and played with) versus being able to name items from a flash card (as is often done in other autism therapies). The staff were experienced, loving, and honoring. They weren't afraid of children like Andrew (something we witnessed when we were out in public). They saw each child as unique with great potential for learning and growth. Andrew attended three full days a week while we transitioned him from his home daycare.

We put our trust in this new community of people. We created meaningful programming for Andrew and set achievable goals. The center encouraged a multidisciplinary approach, so we enlisted an occupational therapist and a behavior therapist to work on gross motor planning and fine motor skills, as well as "social play." We continued with communication, working with the SLP we had met through the More Than Words course. We wanted to do whatever we could, *whatever the experts said*, to set Andrew on a trajectory for a functional, successful, meaningful life.

We also enrolled Andrew in our local elementary school, expecting it would be helpful for his development if he could be with "typical" children in a "typical" social learning environment. These were the same children he'd see on walks, at the park, and at the grocery store in our community.

Andrew attended both places part-time. The schedule eventually became routine, me carting Abby along to either the autism center or our local school. Some days we would walk, Abby old enough to sit up in her stroller, smiling and waving at the people walking by. Andrew walked up ahead, school bag on his back, vocalizing happy sounds as he navigated the familiar route to school.

That year we worked on everything from communication to toilet training to successfully drinking from a glass. (I had worried Andrew would be drinking from a sippy cup for the rest of his life!) He took on all of it.

We helped Andrew desensitize to the sound of Abby's crying. He mastered (a term used by the therapists) putting on his shoes, taking turns, and following a visual schedule. He understood the concept "First . . . Then . . . " used routinely in autism therapy, which meant that when he followed a directive, it led to something positive, like a toy or other "reward." A bit like Pavlov's dog, it was classic autism therapy set in a naturalistic setting, as I understood it.

Over the years we would add goals, modify existing ones, and check off those accomplished from the list. We could see the growth in Andrew's ability, including the improvement in his communication and his behavior. We hoped it felt beneficial to Andrew too. I wanted to maintain all of Andrew's uniqueness while helping him gain skills and learn new ways of managing his world.

Most significant was his emerging ability to communicate. Through a rigorous, repetitive, sequential training program called Picture Exchange Communication System (PECS), Andrew learned, from the age of four, that communicative action created an intended, specific, desired result. That when he brought someone a little one-inch card, on which was a specific picture symbol and word, from a specific page in his binder of symbol cards, his needs would be met, be it a favorite food, a walk outside, or help using the toilet.

It was groundbreaking for our family. Up to that point we had relied on Andrew's sounds and gestures, including taking our hand and bringing it to what he desired, in order to understand what he wanted. Sometimes it was just intuitive. Most parents know what their child wants even before they ask. But this new way to communicate gave Andrew autonomy, a way to participate in his own life. It meant we had additional ways of learning what Andrew needed, beyond guessing or intuition.

Almost instantly, we saw a reduction in meltdowns and aggressive behavior. We saw a happier child. Instead of biting his arm or taking it out on Abby, Andrew could request what he needed. He could participate in a world that wanted to help him. Now, his world understood him.

We used PECS for years, long before we considered using an iPad for communication, as there were meaningful exchanges happening with those one-inch picture squares. Andrew had to initiate. He had to approach us, persist, or learn to wait until he had our attention, and then see that, in doing so, his method worked: he got what he wanted—his needs were met.

Only years later would we trial a device-based communication application (pointing to symbols that produce voice output) that would eventually replace the clunky PECS binder we had become so accustomed to carrying. (We still have the binder. I kept it.

There was so much work and effort in those pages—a symbol, to me, of perseverance: of knowing the power of communication and of what it looks like to never give up.)

It took many months of practice for Andrew to learn the concept of "picture exchange," and his vocabulary of pictures expanded then over the years. He worked hard at learning to communicate and he was "rewarded" for his efforts. In the beginning it came through food—raisins or his favorite snickerdoodle cookie. But over time, the reward became intrinsic—Andrew gained access to the people and places he loved. In return, we were rewarded. We grew to cherish this new dynamic between us. In fact, we came to love those little picture squares, *even if* they got lost in Andrew's pile of books, or under his feet, buried in the garden.

Eventually, we couldn't wait to see what Andrew had to say. Never did a day go by when we weren't grateful for that binder of pictures, ever. It changed our world, and it certainly changed Andrew's.

I remember the first time Andrew gave me the love symbol. Unsolicited, spontaneous. I had been showing it to him for weeks. With a pounding heart and tears in my eyes, I accepted the first "I Love You" from my almost seven-year-old son. In my mind, I could hear him saying it to me. I imagined just how beautiful his voice might be

***

Over the years, we interacted with families who were navigating a similar path to ours. We shared ideas, best practices, therapists, and therapies. We commiserated when things felt tough or laughed at the countless examples of how we had normalized our otherwise fairly unusual family life: keeping multiple copies of favorite books in case one was lost, going to the grocery store only when it was quiet, or having a stash of preferred snacks, "flickers," or other items on hand, in order to prevent a meltdown. (Actually, these strategies are not uncommon practice for families in general!)

Over time, we came to a better place of understanding, acceptance, and even of interest in it all. Andrew was aware, bright, and sensitive, and like many children on the autism spectrum, very in tune, intuitive, and soulful. His brain and body worked differently; hence, Andrew interacted with and experienced the world differently. His reactions were often heightened as his sensory world felt amplified.

My role as Andrew's mother became ensuring that Andrew felt comfortable in his body—that he got outside often, moved his body, ate healthy food, and was around people who loved and accepted him for who he was. I no longer felt that he needed to be "cured" or fixed; he needed to be supported in the best way possible so he could thrive being who he was, who he is.

My holistic mindset was never far from the forefront. I believed wholeheartedly "you are what you eat." With that, I researched various diets and health protocols purporting to reduce the physiological or biomedical factors contributing to what a child diagnosed with autism might experience, be it gastrointestinal distress, neurological flares, or immune dysfunction.

Overall, Andrew was very healthy, but knowing the gut–brain connection to health, I decided to embark on the labor-intensive Gut and Psychology Syndrome (GAPS) healing diet. It involved extensive food preparation, with a focus on healthy fats, no grains, sugars, or processed foods, and even the elimination of many foods I considered healthy.

We followed the GAPS diet for six months. Six months was the minimum amount of time recommended for healing on the diet, the ideal being two years. But with a baby and a busy toddler, six months was my max. Andrew experienced incredible benefit, including improved gut health, which resulted in textbook healthy bowel movements. We saw in him a deeper, more focused connection. Although we weaned him off the very limited GAPS diet, we continued to incorporate many of the healing fats and supplements into Andrew's daily routine. Nutrition would always be a foundational piece to Andrew's health and his ability to thrive.

My view of autism had evolved, though I would always stay close to wanting to understand the root cause of health versus merely treating (or masking) symptoms. I grappled with understanding how someone as beautiful, wise, and *intended* as Andrew could be considered "wrong." *Are we supposed to "prevent" children like Andrew from existing? Would he be who he is without his autism?* My mind was trying to make sense of something that my heart was willing to accept.

I came to understand that autism is an expression of our human genetics—that autistic individuals are a segment of a diverse population. We come into life with a genetic predisposition, a set of possibilities, some more certain than others (like having blue eyes). A variety of factors influence the expression of these genetics, which is what we see manifest as the person we become. Factors such as our mother's health, our father's genetics, and the health of the amniotic environment in utero; internal influences such as inflammation, the microbiome, gut health, metabolic pathways like methylation and detoxification; external influences like environmental pollutants, toxins, and nutrients. All these factors contribute to the development of the whole person: someone may have a resilient constitution or a more sensitive one; they may be prone to allergies or heart issues; they may be athletically inclined, artistic, or autistic. And then, of course, *our own* genetics *and* our gut microbiome affects our neurology, our senses, our preferences, and our health functions. It becomes an interwoven, complex feedback system that influences and modulates all of who we are and how we "present." Even the variation within the autistic population shows there are many factors involved. Children without speech have a vastly different set of strengths and challenges (often tied to apraxia—a difficulty or inability to execute motor functions) than autistic children who speak.

Are the rates of autism increasing because these influential factors are increasing, or because our genetics are evolving, or both? Or are there reasons we're still discovering, reasons we're still learning about, perhaps outside of our current mental framework? Is it possible to be autistic and not be burdened by difficult and hindering characteristics, such as sensory over-whelm, repetitive behavior, and obsessive thoughts that are perhaps a result of, or exacerbated by, specific physiologic, metabolic, and neurologic-related imbalances? Can we alleviate these symptoms by supporting the root health of the individual, allowing them to thrive being who they are? Yes, I believed all of this was possible. This is where my holistic perspective would sit.

For me, autism became an opportunity to see that how we live, and how we view health, has an impact on our body, our mind, our world, our children, and ourselves.

After years of seeking out a more positive, holistic, and like-minded perspective on autism, I found the people and resources that matched my values and ideals. It felt comforting and mean-ingful to see autism not as something negative (albeit, still difficult at times), but as an opportunity to grow personally—and to see my child as *intended*, full of possibility and purpose.

I started noticing a greater acceptance in those around us. One afternoon, standing with Andrew at his favorite spot on the riverbank, a kind gentleman strolled by, stopped, and stood with us. He whispered, "He hears things . . . he is more marvelous than any of us . . . " and then walked away. *Odd?* I was moved. Life mirrors back what we hold to be true.

With all the supportive programs, therapies, and health interventions, Andrew seemed to be settling in his body, growing into his own skin, so to speak. He was less reactive and more communicative; he was a happier, good-natured kid. Even Abby was connecting more with Andrew.

The early challenges had lessened as our level of acceptance and understanding grew.

And then we moved.

***

After years of withstanding an unreliable commute on public transit from our suburban home into downtown Toronto's financial district, Stuart became a lesser version of himself. He was tired, worn down, and bitter, traveling most days for a total of three hours. I watched as his weekly grind took its toll on him.

He began mentioning a desire to move into the city, closer to work, to have what he thought were more options: he could walk to the subway, or drive, or even ride his bike when the weather was good. *That all sounds great for him, but what about us?* Our whole life was in the cozy outskirts of the city: the kids' schools, our supports, and most of my friends. The neighborhood had been good to us. How could we leave?

One stressful day, after the commuter train was canceled due to frozen tracks and having waited on the cold platform for nearly an hour, Stuart called and yelled, "We're moving! We have to look at moving. This is killing me." And it was. I could finally see that. And so, we did. We moved.

Sometimes change is good.

We moved to a larger home in the north part of Toronto. The neighborhood was lovely, with big old trees and safe streets for walking. It was just a few blocks from Yonge Street, one of Canada's oldest and longest thoroughfares, and close enough to most major commuter highways, so getting out of the city would be easy too.

Though our home was on a busy street, the lot was big enough that we could sit on the front steps and watch the cars go by or run around and play in the back. Stuart had eyed the lot for its ability to house a pool; he wanted to ensure that Andrew could continue swimming, something he had learned to do and enjoy at our previous house.

For consistency during the transition, we kept both kids at their respective schools in our old neighborhood: Andrew at the autism center (now a thirty-minute drive) and Abby at her preschool, which was just around the corner from Andrew.

The kids managed this huge life change, but did I? Now on the road four times a day, driving back and forth to drop off and pick up, I was feeling ungrounded. We listened to audiobooks and music. Some days I packed my gym clothes to exercise at the local gym in our old neighborhood. I brought my nutrition work and wrote content for my online programs. *But every day? How long can I sustain this?* It wore me down, and although I was happy to support my children through this transition, something had to give.

I did it for nine months. Within a year, I had Abby attending the local elementary school. And just north of us was another elementary school that had a "special education" classroom for children with communication and support needs. I registered Andrew there part-time, driving him after I dropped Abby off at school. He continued part-time at the autism center north of the city (where he'd been attending for three years already), so he could maintain some familiarity within his week.

Eventually, I arranged for a disability transit company to bring Andrew home. It was all a juggle, but it worked. We were making friends and enjoying the new neighborhood. We were still close to both sets of grandparents, which felt important. We were happy, and Stuart was even happier.

In the end, this would be a really good move for our family. It would bring forth meaningful friendships for Abby, Stuart, and me, support and esteem for Andrew within the community, and would reveal a critical path of advocacy that lay ahead.

This is when the stories began to unfold. The story of our family's life, the triumph, the growth. We could see it; we would watch as our story showed up in front of us. All the joy and all the challenge. There was still so much ahead.

"A BEAUTIFUL EXPERIENCE
IS TO BE ABLE TO HAVE
SOMEONE BE WITH ME
IN MY SILENCE."

-ANDREW

CHAPTER 9

One bright, cheery morning, as I dropped Andrew off at the autism center, I was struck by all I had learned about my autistic son. All that was said and not said. All that was felt.

Andrew is very aware; he always has been—aware of what's happening, aware of what's around him, aware of others' presence. Aware and connected. It may not look like it, but anyone who has spent time with Andrew knows this to be true. In fact, you can *feel* it.

He doesn't connect through the usual wave or deliberate hug; it's less overt than that. You might not even know it's going to happen. It's unexpected. It happens when he walks beside you and takes your hand. It happens when he "randomly" touches your face or brushes your shoulder. When he sits on your lap or edges right up beside you. Perhaps he'll stand near you and hum his musical sounds. It seems arbitrary, but it's all intentional. He knows you're there.

He catches your gaze—locks eyes with you—and when that happens, it's like a thousand sparks to your soul. It goes right through you, right to the center of you, right to your heart.

You *feel* it because there's nothing else, no words, no formal exchanges. Just presence. A feeling. Maybe the human connection is a feeling.

I admit that autism—no, Andrew—has taught me *just that*: to connect in the moment and *feel* it. Maybe that moment feels like love, or anger, or hurt. Maybe this is what being human is all about? Not money, or titles, or trophies. Not niceties and norms. Not who you are or what you say, but what you *feel* with someone else. Maybe that's what it is to connect. A feeling. A feeling beyond words.

For as long as I've known Andrew, I've been trying to see life through his eyes. It means tuning in, observing, listening. Sometimes it's intuitive, like when I can just tell that there's too much talking, and I imagine he's spinning in circles because he wants to yell "Please be quiet!" but he can't. Sometimes I laugh, thinking that he'd probably say "This again, Mom?" when I make my routine meals each week. He's witty and clever. You can see it.

Sometimes, though, it takes detective work, like when he throws a book in frustration, or when he hits you and you think, *What the heck, buddy?* And you peel back the layers to realize that no one asked him if *he* was ready to go, or what music *he* felt like listening to, or how *he* felt about having people over. No one asks and he doesn't get to tell you. You've got to see life through *his* eyes.

If we *did* see life through Andrew's eyes, I imagine it might look something like this:

You're all far too busy. What are you so busy doing? Much of what consumes you doesn't really matter. Mom, it doesn't. Get back to what matters. Be kind, kinder, including to your world. Be still. You need to be still or you'll miss it all. It's all right in front of you and within you. It's within me too. I've got thoughts, ideas, and opinions. Believe in me. Believe in everyone. Believe in what you can't see. And if you'd just stop talking, I could hear you. And I think you'd hear me too.

There are many times when we *are* too busy.

I remember the day when my jaw dropped at hearing my own words: "I can't play right now, Andrew. Maybe later." Five or six years prior, I would have begged for Andrew to spontaneously engage with me, to ask me to play, to show any sign of interest in the world outside of his own. He had brought me a blanket, his way of saying "Come play with me!" yet here I was, declining the offer. A sign of how far we had come.

Andrew has learned that engaging with us is fun. It brings him into connection with us. And clearly, I must expect that there will be other offers to play in the future. Other opportunities, other shared moments together.

Most seasoned parents would quickly respond by saying, "Oh my goodness, no big deal! You can't play with your kids all the time." If you're an autism parent, though, you know just *how big a deal* this actually is, to have your child move out of their world and into yours, to ask to engage with you.

In fact, I stopped what I was doing and cried silent tears of joy: *My child wants to play with me! He's asking me to play!* Monumental, massive, incredible. Years of working to create joint interests had reaped benefits.

Life used to be very lonely. My heart used to ache for wanting so badly to be more engaged with my child, to join him in his world, and he, in mine. I would have accepted anything. So, a blanket? Yes I'd take it, absolutely!

Did I wish Andrew played with other kids? Played board games? Did more with us? Yes. And did Andrew wish for these too? Or maybe, some things of *us*? Probably. In fact, I'm sure of it. I trusted we would get there.

In the meantime, we were in a good place.

"MAMA,
WE'RE SHARING LOVE."
–ABBY

CHAPTER 10

Abby's beautiful place in our family is like watching a work of art transform on a canvas, becoming more breathtaking, more stunning, over time. She brings color and vibrancy, playfulness and softness, enhancing the richness and the beauty of those around her. Oh, and with a splash of sass too!

Abby is so clearly meant to be here.

We had always wanted another child after losing James. There was a time when others were cautious for us, perhaps especially once it became clear that Andrew was on a different path.

"Oh! You decided to have another child after Andrew? Weren't you afraid?" said a stranger to me one day at a park while Andrew was playing. I stood there, dumbfounded, with my newborn in my arms. *Afraid? Afraid of having another child who is different, perhaps? Afraid of having hope after loss and grief?*

"No," I said. "We knew we wanted another."

It was the truth. As I looked down at my beautiful baby girl, my faith and trust in the process of life (including the hardship) was clear. *That's why* there are new beginnings. *That's why* there is courage. *That's why* there is Abby.

Abby is the light that shone through the darkness. She will forever be a reminder to us that joy is available, even after pain.

We hadn't known this kind of connection before. A bond unlike Andrew's, Abby is responsive, engaged, and commanding of our attention.

When Abby was a baby, however, her cries would go right through Andrew. You could tell he cared, but he was overwhelmed. The love Andrew had for his sister ran deep, though, and I could tell that, at times, like when he smiled at her, he even enjoyed her company. She knew this—this, the brother who swatted at her if she sucked her thumb, the one who largely ignored her in pursuit of other interests. But never for lack of love. Perhaps for lack of knowing how to express, how to join her world, how to manage her energy in his already oversensitive world.

Living with autism has been challenging—for Andrew and for us. He is good-natured, affectionate, and a good listener, but he speaks a different language, and he often has a different agenda. Transitions are hard, waiting is hard, and when he's *done*, he's done.

It's not that I feel sorry for Andrew or for us, I just wish the journey wasn't so hard. I'm realizing, though, that this is where life's greatest learning and growth occurs, in the hardest parts. I would never have learned my strength as a person, nor my ability to trust my gut to make decisions for my children, were it not for this journey. I expect it will only get stronger. I expect the relationship between Abby and Andrew will get stronger too.

Theirs is a delicate but forgiving flower. Trampled, yet still blooming. One that stands the test of time, blossoming again and again, maybe even out of harsh conditions or from moments least expected.

"Mama! We're sharing love!" Abby said to me from the back seat of our car one day. She was sitting beside Andrew, one car seat apart, with her hand in his. I was as surprised as she was. It was beautiful. Andrew was not only tolerating it, he was happy.

Abby brings pure love to her family. She can't help it; it pours out of her. She has only ever known a brother to be Andrew, in all that he is. Her view is transparent, uncomplicated, and truthful.

When Abby was five, she came home with a painting from art camp. Instructed to draw a conversation between two people, she drew one between her brother and herself–except that Andrew doesn't speak.

"Wow, Abby! That's amazing! What's this about?"

"Well, that's Andrew making his sounds, 'Mmmm mmm mmmmm,' and that's me," Abby said as she showed me her picture. (She had drawn little voice bubbles above herself and Andrew in the picture.)

"And you're saying, 'Why can't you talk, Andrew?'" I said.

"Yes, because he can't talk yet. The teacher helped me spell it out."

And that was that.

Over the years, I've had to explain to Abby (and to other children) that Andrew's body works differently. He understands everything, but his body has trouble making words.

Abby's ability to see things for what they are, to see Andrew for who he is, is refreshing. It's a reminder that sometimes that's all there is to it, that love can be as simple as that; it's a great example to us adults who complicate love, putting conditions on it and boundaries around it.

Abby shows us how to rewrite the definition of love, of relationship, and of what true acceptance looks like. Who says it needs to involve speech? Not Abby. Theirs is a language beyond words.

***

Abby learned about James when she was five. James was her "other brother," she would say.

She had unintentionally come across a picture of me holding James in the NICU. It's what led to me having to explain to Abby that "Mommy had another baby"; "Before you, Abby"; "No, he doesn't live somewhere else." She laughed when I told her that Baby James had to go to heaven.

She was perplexed: "He died? But babies don't die . . . "

And so I told her what I had come to learn from that one week with James: that life isn't a "ticket to one hundred." Some of us live to ninety-seven, or live seven years, or seven days, like James.

It's not what Abby wanted to hear, nor is it what most of us want to believe. But it's just how it is. Love and loss can be extremely painful.

It didn't make sense to Abby, but on some level, she knew it to be true. I explained to her that we could go through life protecting ourselves from the pain of getting close to someone and then losing them, but then we risk losing out on love.

I'm not sure she understood, but one morning, sitting at the kitchen table before school, Abby asked me, "When is James's birthday, Mama?"

My heart skipped a beat. "September twenty-third, Abby." It was within weeks.

"And how old will he be, like, in heaven? And who will celebrate with us? I'll make him a card. What color was his hair? And what about his skin? He lives in heaven now, Mama, right? I wonder what he's doing."

I answered her questions, one by one, my chest tight, my eyes welled up with tears. It was a good thing. Never before had

I talked about James in such a simple way; it was actually a very beautiful perspective.

"So I guess I have two brothers!" she proclaimed. "Ha!" She smiled, very pleased. Then she gently added, "He can breathe now, Mama."

She takes my breath away with her words. "Yes, Abby, you're right, he probably can."

In all of life's busyness, I don't reflect much on James. I don't talk about him with Stuart. I don't think much about that time in our life. And not in an act of avoidance; time just moves you forward.

I feel sad sometimes, worrying the memory of James may grow dim. James's ashes sit in an unassuming, beautiful small wooden box in our dining room. I walk by it every morning, as I turn on the lamp that sits beside him, and every evening, as I turn it off. I know he's there; he'll always be there.

James's life was a hugely significant part of mine. Every year, at his birthday, I reflect on how James's seven days shaped who I became: strong, resilient, and deeply human.

Sometimes I wonder what life would have been like with him in it. Who would he be? What would his face look like? How would his voice sound? What kind of brother would he be to Andrew? Perhaps through Abby's interest in her "other brother," I'll be able to revisit James more. Perhaps, even, one day through Andrew.

***

I could see the relationships developing, evolving, in our family. Andrew and I have always had a deeply rooted bond. Right from his birth, I can remember holding him in my arms, looking deep into his eyes, and *knowing* him. Andrew was very attached to me for the first twelve months of his life, so Stuart had less of this opportunity.

Over time, Stuart developed a playful relationship with Andrew, but it became clouded by autism. What would it look like to be Andrew's dad down the road? Would Stu take him to Scouts? Play catch? Go for bike rides? Cycling was Stuart's passion; sharing that with Andrew would be a dream come true.

We decided that teaching Andrew to ride a bike was worth a shot. Knowing how difficult motor planning was for Andrew, this would be a labor of love. It would require teaching Andrew's body, in sequential steps, the various elements to riding a bike: balance, motion, and coordination. No small feat!

We had been out for bike rides plenty of times as a family. First, Andrew on a tricycle, then a trail-a-bike on the back of Stuart's bike, and then a bike with training wheels. Andrew had learned to pedal and seemed quite comfortable. We figured Stuart would be a natural at teaching Andrew to ride a bike, with his experience and passion for cycling. What we didn't recognize was the utter patience it would require.

Sometimes, when something is so close to your heart, the risk of failure or disappointment can hurt too much. Not to mention that when Andrew was little and still on training wheels, Stuart took him out for a bike ride when Andrew clipped the edge of a curb with his wheel and fell awkwardly to the ground. Andrew was okay, but his bike crushed his forearm, resulting in two broken bones and a dislocated elbow. It was traumatic for Stu; he replayed the crash in his mind for weeks. So, when it became apparent what was truly at stake, I took over.

Methodically, I envisioned the process. I assumed that the most important first step would be for Andrew to achieve comfort and balance on the bike *without training wheels*. We lowered his seat, took the training wheels *and* the pedals off, and created what was essentially a "run bike"–the kind they make for toddlers for this exact reason: to learn to balance and move on a bike. Once Andrew mastered walking with a bike between his legs, we raised his seat. Now he had to move the bike forward while sitting *on* the bike seat, the bike tipping slightly from side to side. Amazingly, he mastered this. In a series of next steps, we went from standing upright, to running up and down the driveway while sitting on the seat, to cruising through the streets in our neighborhood, to balancing on the seat and creating forward motion just with his feet.

I remember the day I knew he was ready. It was Thanksgiving in Canada. "I think we should try it," I said to Stuart. We put his pedals back on, brought him to a quiet stretch of street, held the back of his seat, and, like all parents do, ran beside him before we finally let him go.

I will never forget the sheer joy I felt watching Andrew take off on his own. We were mesmerized, Abby, Stuart, and me. Andrew, too, though he was focused on staying upright!

I was silent, choking back tears, until I finally let out a squeal, so overcome with joy for my child.

"You're doing it, Andrew! You're riding a bike!" I shouted with glee, my smile so wide my face hurt.

Unless you live this life, I'm not sure anyone would fully understand the magnitude of this accomplishment. This was a big deal.

It was a big deal for Andrew, a big deal for his body to master, having always been challenged by getting it to do what he wanted. (At that age, he had yet to hold a pencil and write a single letter, or do up his laces or maneuver a button on his shirt.)

It was a big deal for us. As parents, you run the risk not only of injury to your child but also of the emotional devastation of *What if . . .*

What if my child doesn't get it? What if he never gets it? What if he never progresses from where he is now?

What if he does?

It's hard being the parent of an autistic child who doesn't speak. It's tireless. It's emotional. When we came home that day after seeing Andrew riding his bike on his own, I burst into tears at the absolute pride of it all. Pride and recommitment, because this was the message my brain sent to my heart that day amid the tears: Never, ever give up on your child, even when it's hard, even when you question what they're capable of learning, even when you wonder what lies ahead or if it would be easier to just give up. Never give up on your child because the rewards are beyond what you can only imagine.

Was Stu proud? Absolutely, mostly for Andrew. Stuart knows the joy and freedom that can be experienced free-riding on a bike. Now, this was something they could do together.

Abby? She was beyond excited for Andrew. "We will always remember that Andrew learned to ride his bike on Thanksgiving Day!"

And Andrew? It's hard to say; the look on his face was one of pure concentration. Hopefully, riding a bike gave him a sense of freedom, a sense of unity with his body and power over his life. One day, maybe we'd find out.

***

We had come really far in our acceptance of who Andrew was, but sometimes Andrew's total lack of speech would make me so frustrated, I would be brought to tears. In truth, though, I am amazed at what *can* be communicated without a single word, just by tuning in.

One typical fall afternoon, Andrew *told* me he wanted to go for a bike ride. How? He sat on his bike and waved. I laughed. We ventured out. He told me when he wanted to go straight. He told me which streets he wanted to turn down. He even told me he wanted to move from the road to the sidewalk. How did I know? All without words, with hardly a sound. Mostly, just with his eyes, his smile (which often indicates yes), or his best approximation of no ("nah").

Sometimes I loved our silence. (Life with a very talkative little girl reminded me of this!) Mostly, I was awed by our ability to navigate each day, each month, year after year, with only so much as a few pictures and sounds.

One day he may speak, but we've let that go. We had to. We had to accept that this was our life, that this was our son. That we were meant to go deeper into a world of communication that would show us our capacity for patience, resourcefulness, and true, unconditional love.

I knew Andrew's favorite foods, his favorite color, and that he loved me. Just the same as with Abby. How did I know? Beyond words.

Andrew's world has always been one of senses, of unspoken observation and knowing. His expression of happiness or frustration is much more reflective of the true emotion than the words "happy" or "angry." He doesn't have to say it; he sounds it!

Sound is his whole world. Andrew will listen to anything, even if it doesn't make a sound: a leaf, a pine cone, a piece of fabric. I'm certain he hears things we can't hear. He loves when we sing songs to him, tipping his head to one side, his ear upward as though to catch the notes. There are frequencies he tunes into, I'm sure of it, that bring him pleasure and curiosity.

We used to whimsically sing songs about his day: "Let's put your shoes on, shoes on, Andrew . . . " Abby did too. He would smile. He was tuning in. He loved his family, gave hugs often, and wanted people to sit beside him when he was reading through his *National Geographic* magazines or his books with real pictures and beautiful colors.

Andrew is bright, playful, and loveable. If you ask his nana, she'll tell you that his wit and cleverness has been there right from the start. To me, it is fascinating to think that there is someone *in there*, busy learning and taking in the world, hearing it all. Bit by bit, we are getting to know him more.

What has autism done for us? It has forced us to lean into what really matters: love. It has pushed me to have more trust and faith in the process of life, including in the unknown.

Autism has begged me to ask myself, *Can I be okay having a child who's different? Like, really be okay with it?* It wasn't always a given, but I've learned that I do have the courage to be Andrew's mom.

Autism has faced me with the challenge of truly being okay with who I am, that I don't have to be perfect or always get it right. Andrew is the best example of what it looks like to truly embody who you are. He has taught me that it is possible to experience joy in life by just *being*.

Because of this journey, I take the time to hear the sound of silence, to see the wind in the leaves, and to live more in the moment. Because of this journey, I have learned the value of listening more than speaking. Because of Andrew, I don't take as much for granted and I cherish the little things, like watching him take off his socks, or put a basketball into the net, or when he looks at something and then looks at me in joint recognition.

Through being a mother, I am learning that life does not take a straight path. And that, though there will be ups and downs, many of which will feel impossible to surmount, I am learning I am capable. I am learning that this life can be fun. It is full of treasures; look at the gifts that Abby has brought too.

So I began to wonder: *Can autism be okay? Can we embrace neurodiversity? When a family receives an autism diagnosis, can they be given hope as opposed to a dead-end path? Can they be told about the joy that will come, not just the challenge?* Yes, there are ways we can support the autistic body and mind so that the challenges are lessened, but I can honestly say, I look forward to the future, to learning more about Andrew.

You see, I am inspired by autistic people and their stories. I am inspired by Andrew. And sometimes I'm even inspired by our own family's life. Deep down, I know there is so much more ahead: for our family, for me as a mother, for Abby, Stu, and for Andrew.

"BE WITH THOSE WHO LIFT YOU UP.
INVEST IN THINGS THAT MATTER—
NATURE, TREES, AIR, MUSIC, BOOKS
THAT OPEN YOUR MIND AND HEART.
NOW IS THE TIME, NOT LATER."

-ANDREW

CHAPTER 11

As a family, our goal has been to lead by example. Stuart and I have wanted to show Abby and Andrew what being a loving family *with autism* looks like. In turn, we have shown our community.

When Andrew and Abby were younger and we did things together that could otherwise be difficult or awkward because of the set of challenges that autism brought, like exploring a new playground or going out to a restaurant (infrequent as that was), we showed ourselves and others that diversity in our community *includes* disability. We can't hide who we are, so we bring autism along with us.

One winter Stuart decided that our family should "get into skiing." It would help break up the long winter months. Friends had recommended a family-friendly ski hill one hour north of the city for kids' weekend lessons. Stuart was game. Andrew would enjoy the drive. We'd go for the morning and stay for lunch.

We enrolled Abby in lessons with a few friends and we pursued adapted ski lessons for Andrew. Stuart and I would meet Andrew's instructors, teach them everything they needed to know about him (how he communicates with noises, gestures, and a few picture symbols—All Done, Toilet, and Mom—that we had affixed to a key-ring loop on his snow pants), then we'd ski together with them for a bit as they practiced zigzagging down the learner's hill.

Stuart and I were thrilled, and not because we needed Andrew to "get it," but because we were free! Andrew was looked after and Abby was fine. Stuart and I would take off and ski together. What a luxury! It felt exhilarating and fun. We felt no guilt in having that time together doing something we both enjoyed.

Our experience was positive, and the more positives we gained, the more confident we became to try new things.

Enter: snow tubing.

Instead of signing Andrew up for weekly private lessons, we gave him alternate weeks off. We would still go up as a family, Abby had her group ski lesson with friends, and Stuart and I would do something different with Andrew, like go for a hike nearby.

One week I had the idea to try tubing. We had gone tobogganing before, so I knew that Andrew was used to the sensation of sliding down a hill with speed. Plus, I loved tobogganing, so I was up for this new adventure. Stuart could ski with the other parents while Abby was in her lesson.

What ensued was a comedic episode of mishap, perseverance, and love. So meaningful was our experience that I wrote about it and shared it in a letter to the ski hill. The letter was posted to the ski hill's Facebook page. The story took off, catching the attention of hundreds, then thousands, online. The opportunity for Andrew to impact the lives of many had begun.

To the staff at the Snow Valley Tube Park in Barrie working the Sunday morning shift on February 5, 2017:

Thank you.

Thank you for pausing the rope tow a thousand times for Andrew.

Thank you for remaining calm when Andrew rolled out of his tube, again and again, on the many attempts to get him up to the top that first time.

Thank you for not making us feel bad that thirty-plus people were waiting in line while we created a holdup for what felt like an eternity.

Thank you for working with us, not against us, to figure it out.

Thank you for doing your job and for showing others how it's done: treating people with dignity and respect, no matter what.

And thank you to the staff who ran up the length of the hill, alongside Andrew sitting in his tube, coaching him to stay in the tube, and cheering when he finally, successfully, got to the top. Thank you for letting me hug you, overcome with my own emotions.

Your efforts paid off, you see, because once he got it, he got it for good. I couldn't wipe the smile off his face (his cheeks must have hurt), and the look of pride and glee was unmistakable.

And now you've met Andrew and you've been given one of the gifts of autism: the chance to rise up and choose to experience patience, tolerance, compassion, and love.

At the end of five rides, I hugged Andrew so hard and mouthed the words "I'm so proud of you"-only because I was too choked up to actually speak.

It's not a lack of belief in his ability; it's an acknowledgment of the effort that's required on his part (and mine) to overcome obstacles. To persevere. And to shine a light for others to see the ability in disability.

Thank you for your part in today.

Susan Baker
Andrew's mom

There was a collective applause.

We received hundreds of messages from skiers and families alike, some who knew firsthand the feat of an adventure such as this. There was a camaraderie, an understanding of the joy and challenge of this life. *Perhaps people do know about autism,* I thought. Perhaps they know about the hurdles families face and how discouraging it can feel to face them. Perhaps humanity *is* compassionate and tolerant and understanding. Perhaps there is room for disability, for accommodation, and for Andrew.

Because here's the thing:

As an autism parent, you want it all: compassion, understanding, and acceptance. You want people to see the uniqueness of your child, of your family, but also, to kind of fit in among our differences. You want people to make accommodations for your child, but not out of pity. You want sympathy, but not too much.

We all want these things: compassion, understanding, and acceptance.

Life was feeling up. I felt a renewed commitment, yet again, to my child, to his needs, and to the desires of our family. That we all have a right to access joy and fun and new experiences. But more than anything, I knew that I could do this. I could do this life with autism.

***

In time, I would learn that life with autism (or life with Andrew) would be like that: a series of ups and downs. It would include highs, lows, and plateaus, like riding a roller coaster. A feeling that everything was okay, then a twinge, ever so subtle, as you cautiously look over your shoulder, wondering if something's coming, something hard, something that knocks you off your feet. The feeling of wondering when the other shoe might drop.

I would learn that I could not control what was coming. That the only way I could possibly enjoy this life was to be *in it*–to be in each present moment, for what it was. I would learn this, in time, but not yet. I hadn't learned it yet. All I could feel was the creeping anxiety of something shifting. And something was definitely shifting.

I would run through the list in my mind: *Is it because we moved? Does Andrew not feel well? Is he reacting to something, a change in diet, a new food? Is he growing? Is his body sore? Are there problems at school? Is he unhappy at the autism center or tired of the commute? Tired of gray days? Tired of autism?* Whenever things felt "off," I would run through this list.

We were in Andrew's tough season: cold, dark days with less time outdoors. In winter, it became apparent how desperately Andrew needed to be outside. Something about the lack of sun or its warmth on his skin, we would find there were more crying spells, unprovoked aggressive behavior, and overall discontent.

Nature literally grounds Andrew. He goes barefoot when it is just warm enough to have his feet on the earth. He can spend hours outside. He explores, finding leaves and listening to the sound they make. He is most content when he is in nature. I think we all are. I have never spent so much time in nature as I have since spending time with Andrew.

Grounding, also called "Earthing," is the practice of being in direct (skin) contact with the earth's natural surface (e.g., grass, sand, dirt, water, wood). Doing so discharges inflammation, or stress, from our physical body. According to the book *Earthing* (2014) by Clinton Ober, Stephen T. Sinatra, MD, and Martin Zucker, our bodies are bioelectric–most processes, signals, and messages in and between our cells occur through electrical transmission—and the earth's natural electric charge helps our body establish its most natural, healthy electric state. This is literally called "being grounded." It can positively affect mood, energy, and sleep.

Stuart and I view being outside as prescriptive: it is essential for Andrew, and all of us, to have a daily dose of fresh air, to move our bodies, and to keep our eyes wide open to the elements. We all benefit. It's not that winter makes us feel isolated. It's that the better weather makes being outside that much more accessible: we eat outside, play outside, and live outside. Much of that is missing in the short days of winter. Still, we persevere. And if ever I forget how important it is, Andrew is the first to remind me.

What started as an attempt to take Andrew to the zoo one gray day, late winter, ended in a hike at a random river trail instead. Andrew was off from school. We had a season's pass to the Toronto Zoo, not because Andrew liked animals, but because it gave us an outing: we could go for a drive, walk around the zoo grounds, and be outside.

That day we got as far as the parking lot. I could just tell something was amiss. After I parked and unbuckled Andrew, he ran out of the car, crying. He lunged at the car beside us, reaching up to its windshield where he grabbed the wiper blade, almost ripping it off. No one was in the car, but still, I felt angry with Andrew and resentful; so much of my time was devoted to making (or keeping) Andrew happy, yet sometimes it felt like it was all in vain. Sometimes it's just downright hard. We left immediately, both of us in tears.

What happened next only happened because I needed a plan B, not because I was astute or wise. It would, though, become the training ground for understanding Andrew's deep need for nature.

As we drove away from the zoo, my face hot with anger, Andrew still crying, I swore I would drive until I ran out of gas. I wanted to be alone, isolated, and safely contained in the confinement of the car. What I realized was that we were driving by acre upon acre of forested land, a vastness that suddenly appealed to me.

At what looked like a trail entrance, I pulled the car over, parked, and let Andrew run into the woods. I followed. What presented was one of the most peaceful and enjoyable times I'd had with Andrew in a long while.

The dense forest filled the air with scents of cedar and pine. We could hear the trickle of a stream and feel our quiet footsteps on the forgiving forest floor. I found myself singing–familiar folk songs, then church songs with lyrics I remembered from when I was a child. Andrew, up ahead, his demeanor completely changed, now laughing and content, would turn and pause, saying "mah" for more. He was listening. And he had a favorite: "Make Me a Channel of Your Peace." Quite a beautiful song, actually. Quite a beautiful turn of events.

I had let go. I often have in my mind what I think life should look like, what I think we *should* be doing, but that day I was forced to do it differently. It's not easy for me, but that day it led to something much more beautiful than anything I had planned.

Life showed me a different path. It led me to understanding that I would need to be flexible and open, especially as life with Andrew was shifting. It was becoming clearer that Andrew couldn't tolerate busy spaces or places where he just didn't want to be. The sooner I could let go of expectations, the sooner I would be shown the possibilities of what lie ahead.

It was also the end of the zoo and the beginning of hundreds of forest walks. The forest would become a place of solace, joy, and exploration for Andrew. Some of our most meaningful experiences with Andrew, and with our family, would come out of a forest.

"GRATITUDE IS
TO GIVE YOUR ATTENTION
TO WHAT MATTERS."
-ANDREW

CHAPTER 12

Like an intricate web, as one family member shifts, everyone shifts. It was no different with Abby. She was observing the dynamic of Andrew within our family, and as she got older, she began to notice how her brother was, in fact, *different*. Then she cried for the first time at having "a brother like Andrew."

We were at a community event. Upon leaving, Andrew rolled in the grass, happy and vocal. As we got in the car, I noticed Abby's demeanor had changed. She looked quiet and distraught.

"What's your face, Abby?" (An expression we use in our house.)

"Nothing," Abby replied, arms crossed, disgruntled.

"Oh . . . because it seems like something just happened. Your face changed."

And she burst out: "I feel so embarrassed when Andrew throws himself on the ground and makes his loud sounds! Other kids don't do that! I don't always want to be the sister of Andrew like that!" She was upset and crying.

"I'm sorry, Andrew," she said to him. "I know you are just being you. But it was embarrassing and I don't always like it."

And there it was, my bright, beautiful girl, feelings collided: embarrassment and then guilt for feeling that way. I could tell her tears were beyond anger; she felt bad for admitting it at all.

"Oh, baby girl. I hear you. You can let it out, even with Andrew here. He understands. Of course it's hard for you sometimes. It's okay to feel that way. It used to be for me, too, you know. I used to feel embarrassed. And then I would feel bad. Andrew knows this. You can talk about it."

It felt awkward to talk about Andrew with him right there, especially knowing he understands, but it *is* our reality. I told myself: If this was an argument, or any other sibling interaction, we'd have to work it out in the moment. This was no different. So, there we were, sitting in the car, putting it all out there. Honest, raw, and real.

I knew this day would come. The day when Abby needed support, when she needed to hear words I couldn't give her. The day she would need to be with people who "get it," just like her. A month later, Abby walked out of her first support group for siblings of kids with "special needs." She was beaming.

"Mama! You won't believe this! I met a girl who is the same age as me, *and* her birthday is in January, *and* she has a brother with autism. The only thing that's different is that her brother is also in a wheelchair. But otherwise, we're basically the same!"

She was so happy, she was flying. I imagine it's much like how I feel when I am with like-minded people, or when I connect with parents and moms, walking a similar path to mine, navigating life with a child with significant needs. You feel validated, seen, and heard.

Month after month, Abby attended the sibling meetups and looked forward to spending time with kids who had a life like hers. One month the facilitator guided them through talking about how the sibling relationship is the longest lasting of all, something to which I, myself, had not given much thought. She came out of the meeting and pronounced:

"Okay, Andrew, we're going to be brother and sister for a long time. So let's make a deal: I'll take care of you, and you take care of me, for the rest of our life, okay? Deal? Deal." And they shook on it. Abby asked Andrew to hold her hand, which he did, smiling, and that was the deal. Signed, sealed, delivered.

Sitting in the back seat, of course, they couldn't see the tears streaming down my face, or hear my heart skip a beat, or see my lips whisper a silent, "Thank you for my Abby."

Though life continues to shift in ways I can't predict, I am shown the incredible richness that comes out of the unexpected.

***

I realized that I was headed toward depletion.

Years of holding it together after a diagnosis, appointments, and therapies, not to mention the loss of one child and the birth of another, I was run ragged. The recent shift in Andrew's behavior had added to the drain, but this felt older than that. This felt familiar. My modus operandi, my MO, was catching up to me.

For as long as I could remember, I had felt overwhelmed. Not that anyone would have noticed; it ran as a back current, like a default. I would get overwhelmed by all I said yes to, but also by my responsibilities. "A full plate," my mom would say. Overwhelmed by being *busy*, the busyness coming from a place of always needing to feel productive in order to feel *of value*–including to myself. Sometimes I would even feel overwhelmed by my own passion and ideas. I love life; I get really *into it*. It's hard for me to slow down, to be still and just *be*.

I connect with this busy state of being. It's *me*. I created much of my success as a nutritionist this way, teaching, delivering corporate nutrition seminars, mentoring fellow nutritionists and hosting monthly meetings with guest speakers, all while juggling my own private practice. But it goes further back than that.

As a little girl, I wanted to please my parents by getting the best grades, being involved in school, and keeping the peace around the home, making sure that everyone was okay. I didn't know it then, but that same behavior, that same zest for life, would one day stop me in my tracks and force me to do things differently.

I carried this pulse into my role as a spouse and as a mother. Passionate yet intense. Committed yet vigilant.

This pattern of constant drive and production, coupled with an analytic and creative personality, along with *my own* sensory challenges of a bright and busy world, equates to a vivacious but stretched-thin human. Me.

It's a place of emotional exhaustion, that place where you've got nothing left to give. You can't pour from an empty cup. How could I be any good to my children when I was grinding myself down? I couldn't.

Like a foreshadowing, I knew I needed to take care of myself. I couldn't afford to burn out. Life could get harder, my anxious brain would worry.

Walking my talk as a holistic nutritionist, I took care of myself physically, mentally, and emotionally. I ate well. I was on supportive supplements for my nervous system and stress hormones. I did yoga and I moved my body.

But the nourishment needed to go deeper.

I needed space. I needed space for my mind to breathe and my spirit to be reignited. I needed space in my calendar. And so, my own shift began. It was a beginning, a new way of be-ing. Uncomfortable, I knew I needed it. More than that, I needed to believe that it was okay to take care of myself. In fact, it was necessary.

Playfully, I came up with a prescription for myself:

1. Schedule in space, literally, in the agenda.
2. Have more fun. And more often. Make a list to remind you of how to have fun.
3. Spend time with yourself. You've got great insight. Stop long enough to hear it.
4. Stay fiercely committed to your causes, your relationships, your children, and nutrition, including changing the world. Just take it down a notch.
5. Don't laugh at #1–4. Follow. Then repeat.

This felt like me. Friends would remind me that this was who I was. It felt good, but would it bring me back to myself and out of depletion? Time would tell.

"OUR STORIES
NOURISH THE SOUL
IN ALL OF US."
-SUSAN

CHAPTER 13

We were all at home when I exploded. What were we doing anyway? The details never seemed to matter. It was after supper, a cool late-spring evening. The smell of pre-summer warmth was in the air. We were in the kitchen, cleaning up, the kids lingering at my feet. I felt smothered. Like a pot boiling over, I'd reached my limit. I needed to leave.

There was nowhere to go—nowhere I wanted to go—except out, away from it all, away from autism. I ran into the backyard, into our garden at the back of our fenced property, and I crumbled. Folded in a heap on the ground, my hands in the dirt, I let the cold, dark soil pass between my fingers. Completely overcome by my emotions, I was, suddenly, gardening. I found myself digging, weeding, tossing.

And then words came.

I could hear them. Like a poem, the words echoed in my head. Single words, then chains of words, statements, eventually taking the form of a letter. A letter to my child. An apology letter. An apology letter to my autistic child and the note I imagined he would write to me in return. I ran back inside the house, mumbled to Stuart that I needed a few more minutes, grabbed my phone and ran back outside to the dark, to the quiet, where the words were. I jotted them down in a note.

It was an apology letter to Andrew, from me, his mom. *Imagine.*

It felt so good to write. So cathartic. It was an honest apology through words I couldn't say to my child but that I knew were true, and that he knew were true too.

The words took my breath away—they were so real, so vulnerable. But they stung. I felt sad about this glaring paradox: a deep, intense love for my child against the challenges of a life I, in truth, in that moment, didn't want. I read the words over. They resonated so deeply.

Something in me knew I was not alone in this. Yes, I had Stuart who understood the inner dimensions of this life, but there were others. There had to be. I had to share these words; they were not just for me. I felt certain.

So, with a deep breath and a courageous step, I posted my letter to my Facebook page and then walked away. I walked back into the reality of the life I had just exposed.

Who knew where that letter would go or whether it would reach anyone, but it was the truth, my truth. That's all that mattered.

It read:

> An apology letter to my autistic child and the note
> I imagine he'd write me in return:
>
> Dear Andrew,
>
> I know I don't need to write this, but I'm writing it
> anyway.
>
> I'm sorry.
>
> I'm sorry for all the things I said or did (or didn't
> say or do) when you were first diagnosed with autism.
>
> I'm sorry that things were so tough—for you, for me,
> for all of us. I'm sorry that the road to understanding
> and acceptance was so bumpy.

I'm sorry I yelled at you-screamed, cried, cursed. I'm sorry you had to see the ugly side of me. The human side. The real and honest side.

I'm sorry that sometimes I thought I didn't have the strength to go on.

I'm sorry I ever wanted or wondered, even for a second, what life would be like without you.

I'm sorry for wishing you could talk. And for crying in your face, "Why can't you talk? WHY CAN'T YOU TALK!"

I'm sorry for wondering if you should have more friends. Or even a couple friends.

I'm sorry for wishing you had "normal" interests. Or more interests.

I'm sorry for secretly wishing that maybe you'd be one of those autistic people with a unique or incredulous talent. The ones you hear about. The ones that make headlines. One of those savants. I'm sorry for thinking that somehow this would make the hard worth it.

I'm sorry I didn't always see you for you.

I'm sorry for ever doubting you.

Truth is, I think you're brilliant. I think you're smart, loving, intuitive, funny, and forgiving. I know you're so in there; I know that you understand more than any of us are aware.

I know you're here to show us how to love, how to bring us all back to love.

My life is a thousand times richer because of you.

And I'm so proud of you.

I love you.

Love,
Mom

And just as quickly as the words to *my* letter came, so did a voice with words I imagined to be Andrew's.

Dear Mom,

Thank you.

Thank you for believing in me, for advocating for me, and for seeing me for all that I am (and not just a label).

Thank you for coming into my world and for learning to see the beauty that I see.

Thank you for learning to speak without words, moving from your head to your heart. Thank you for learning my language.

Thank you for dancing with me, singing to me, and for talking to me even when I don't seem to be paying attention. I am.

Thank you for getting to know the things I love: music, books, nature, and walks. And food!

Thank you for allowing me my interests. Thank you for allowing me to be who I am.

Thank you for seeing yourself in me.

Thank you for being my best friend. You understand me more than anyone.

Thank you for not trying to fix me, but rather, support me in all of who I am. Thank you for the research you do, the therapies, and the vitamins (even when I protest). I know your intention is pure.

Thank you for not seeing me as broken.

Thank you for being brave.

I know it was hard for you. It was hard for me too. But all I saw was love, Mom. I could feel that your heart was aching, and that you felt torn and weak at times. But I also felt all the joy. And all I saw was love.

Thank you for never giving up.

I love you too.

Love,
Andrew

The response to the letter was a tidal wave.

Comments from parents who were feeling the same came through in the hundreds. Replies from mothers and fathers of children with exceptionalities and typical children, alike. Messages of compassion, empathy, and relating.

What struck me most was that this was not about autism; this was a universal experience of struggle, sorrow, and a reckoning of our human nature through, in this case, the lens of motherhood.

From pride to guilt to love, the truth of my experience was, on some level, the truth of their experience too. Whether someone had a child diagnosed with autism or not, these parents were identifying with my words, with my vulnerability.

It was the first time I had shared so publicly. Was it an infringement on the trust in my relationship with Andrew? An unsolicited exposure of our relationship? Had I been a traitor to my child? It didn't feel like that. It felt like the first time I had allowed myself the validation of my own experience independent of his.

I never read him the letter (although I did apologize to Andrew, and to Abby and Stuart, for my explosion, after the fact). It felt awkward and I felt embarrassed. I was speaking for him, and on some level, it was what I wanted to believe. I had always spoken for him. In a way, I represented him. After all, I knew him best. Regardless, I was allowed these words; my experience was valid and there was no shame in that.

What was this anyway? This testimony of my experience. This outpouring of camaraderie and community? This bearing witness to our family's journey?

This was life, love, and autism. It was the beginning of me sharing our story. I would share all sides of it: the joy, the hardship, and the triumph. I vowed to myself that I would share the truth.

It wasn't that I felt compelled to write; I felt called. I knew that, by putting words to what I was experiencing, not only would it validate *my* experience but also perhaps that of another. I felt called to show up, maybe so that others would know they were not alone. Maybe so that others could do the same: to show up in *their* life as I was showing up in mine.

This was the power of words.

Sometimes the words aren't for me. Sometimes the words just need to be written. Sometimes I write the words as if no one will read them. I write them when I feel moved to do so. Nothing scheduled or contrived. All from a place of inspired truth.

And so became my online blog, *Life, Love & Autism*.

Week by week, the words came. They came to me when I was driving, working, or in the kitchen snapping green beans. They came out of moments of inspiration or from days of difficulty. I couldn't move forward until I captured the words; they wouldn't leave. They came when there was a story to tell. And so I shared. I shared our life with the world, even if it was awkward or uncomfortable or temporary. I shared because it was real, because life *is* real and hard and beautiful, all at the same time.

***

Things *were* shifting. I had heard that puberty, including the years leading up to puberty, could be very difficult for individuals with autism. Families who had gone through it struggled to describe its impact or what it actually looked like in their life. I expected that, with his hormones fluctuating and physiological changes beginning, Andrew's body would start to feel different. Andrew, so sensitive and acutely aware, would *feel* this affecting his mind, his sensory system, and his body. I expected this could be very uncomfortable for him.

I had such sympathy for Andrew. Even when I was feeling impatient and had had enough, I felt for him. His whole system seemed to be in flux. I could only imagine what was causing him such volatility. We were seeing unprovoked bursts of anger and spontaneous bouts of tears. He would be happy one minute, then banging his head the next. Andrew was becoming more sensitive, more reactive, and less predictable. Intuitive as I had become, I was beginning to fear I was losing touch.

In those days, I would look deep into Andrew's eyes, and I would worry that he was beyond reach. What more could I do? What else could I offer? We were working with a functional medical doctor who specialized in autism. Specific vitamins and supplements had been recommended to support various metabolic functions, such as detoxication and elimination. We made sure he got plenty of time outside to move his body and discharge his energy and emotions. We took him for hikes, bike rides, and car drives. He attended "movement therapy," a brain and body-based form of therapy that, through specific physical movements of the body, brings regulation, integration, and optimization to the brain. He ate well and was still off allergenic foods like gluten and dairy. We had focused on gut health and gut healing. We made sure his water was clean; we went as far as to reduce chlorine exposure from his daily city-water baths by using chlorine filters and detox salts. It felt like we were doing *everything*, but none of it felt like enough.

Our intention was to support Andrew as much as possible through natural means in an effort to avoid medication for as long as possible. Andrew's pediatrician agreed, stating that

Andrew's behavior and challenges were typical of a teen going through puberty and that "even with autism" he would suggest leaving medication as a last resort due to probable side effects. Antipsychotics could help with irritability and aggression, but so could magnesium, L-theanine, and medical cannabidiol or CBD, we learned. We filed this away, knowing that medication was something we could pursue in the future, if needed.

The stress was mounting. My nerves were raw and I was "losing it" on the kids regularly. Completely overwhelmed by weeks of meetings with Andrew's school team, appointments, and therapies, as well as what felt like constant requests from Andrew (for snacks, for the lights to be off, for a walk), I was on edge.

I woke up one morning with a pink raised rash across my neck and face. It was a stress rash, confirmed by my homeopathic doctor, for which he prescribed a remedy. It went away, but the clear message behind it was that I needed to pull back. It felt selfish, but I needed to take the weight of the world off my shoulders.

It had all hit a critical mass. I cried to Stuart: "How are we going to do this? When is this going to get easier? What is our life right now?!"

Stress does that; it magnifies all that's hard and diminishes the view of all that's working. We had our health, we had support and resources, and we had each other. We would be okay, but I couldn't see any of it. I was sick of it all.

I was sick of rushed mornings and stressful bedtimes. I was sick of grocery shopping and cooking. I was sick of birthdays and holidays and presents and store returns.

I was sick of Abby's stories and the guilt I felt about not listening.

I was sick of Andrew's limited interests and his obsession with his iPad (at the time). I was sick of him lunging at me, so overcome by his own emotions. And I was sick of seeing him take it out on Abby.

I was sick of Andrew breaking down in the middle of a store. I was sick of feeling so much rage I could hurt him, sick of denying those feelings, sick of the shame.

I was sick of feeling like I was living in "fight or flight" most of the time. Sick of admitting that perhaps things *really were* tough, but not wanting to expose it for fear that it would cloud someone's view of Andrew. Or of autism. Or of me.

I was sick of arguing with Stuart. Sick of the increased tension and uneasiness in our home.

I was sick of Andrew not talking. I was sick of autism. And I was sick of hating this part of my child when I so desperately wanted to love the whole of who he was.

I was living in two worlds: one that I loved, that inspired me, that felt easy. The one where I made "salads in a jar" with neighbors and hosted community nutrition talks. The one where I was something other than a mom.

The other was one that was hard. One that was rough and dirty. A grind. I loved that one too, but it drained me. It was the one I wanted to give up on, but never would. The one that kept me up at night. The one I couldn't look up in a book, to see how to do it, or what came next, or how it ended.

I was sick of being strong. I wanted people to see me cry—my family, my friends, my online community. I wanted people to see that disability can be hard. That, sometimes, you lose your spirit.

I never, though, wanted people to feel sorry for us. I never wanted them to misinterpret the truth for unhappiness. Because I wasn't unhappy. I loved my children and my life. I was just absolutely sick of it all.

Through focusing more on myself, things turned around, temporarily. I reminded myself that it all starts with me. I told Abby and Andrew that I would practice being more present. I told Stuart I would try to have more laughs. And I told myself I would be gentle and show self-compassion.

From this place, I discovered that I needed to make a shift. I needed quiet time at the start of the day, before anyone awoke, just to collect my thoughts. I couldn't afford to have anyone override my state with their own. So, I needed to wake up at least ten minutes before the household, before the morning flurry began. Ten minutes to sit, breathe, and just be. Eventually, I added in a five-minute gratitude journal. It helped. In fact, I would continue this practice for years to come.

"WHEN LIFE IS HARDEST,
THERE LIES AN OPPORTUNITY
TO DISCOVER WHAT MATTERS."
–ANDREW

CHAPTER 14

I don't know what it was about that one particular day—it was just the day after the last, after all—but it felt different. It felt heavy, ominous. It was dark and gray and cold. A February day in Toronto is like that, but this was different; it *felt* different. It lacked hope.

Andrew had been having a tough time. As usual, I ran the list through my mind: *Is he overtired? Is he reacting to a food? Is he deficient in something, lacking a certain nutrient? Is it preteen hormones? Is it pre-spring allergies? A gut imbalance, an overgrowth of intestinal yeast (common in children diagnosed with autism, often appearing seasonally) that is affecting his mind?* But this felt more significant, more than just a change in season or a rainy day.

That dark, gray February day, eight-year-old Andrew was angry. He had come home from the autism center (where he had been spending most of his days) uptight and spent. Maybe it had been a hard day, maybe a hard week. It certainly was not his best time of year; the long, dark days of winter took their toll on Andrew. He was often agitated and reactive.

Abby was home from school, chattering and lively, unpacking her school bag, marveling at her kindergarten creations. I could feel the tension rising. Like every other day, my job was to monitor Abby's level of exuberance with Andrew's tolerance for it. His sensory world was so saturated and Abby just added to it, joyous or otherwise. Without wanting to squelch Abby's spirit, I would gently dance around her ("Oh that's so lovely, Abby. Tell me how you made that . . . ") in an attempt to usher her into another place, out of Andrew's space.

I would whimsically offer Andrew a snack and smile brightly through a false facade, trying to hide my fear that he was going to blow. It was exhausting. "Keeping the peace," trying to keep everyone happy and everything in order, had become a full-time job. I questioned how much longer I could do it. I was burning out.

Those late-afternoon hours approaching dinner were the hardest. Processing his own day, Stuart would walk into what he called "a crime scene": Andrew jumping around in agitation, biting his wrists, Abby crying, unable to catch her breath, and me, shaking. Stu swore on some days that he'd be better turning around and walking right back out the door. I believed him. Except that we needed him. In those days, we needed each other.

Our arguing increased. Stuart and I argued so much that I thought for sure we were damaging our children. Whether we argued in front of them or behind closed doors, there was no getting away from it. Poor Abby. My heart used to break seeing her so fearful, so worried about her precious family, so desperate because there was nothing her little five-year-old self could do to stop it.

Andrew, though astute, was typically consumed by managing whatever he was experiencing in his own world. I wondered whether our arguing was making things worse for him. Did he know he was the source of our tension?

It was a vicious cycle, fragile and unrelenting, that played out over and over, until one day, that one specific day, it all shattered.

That one tumultuous evening, it reached a tipping point. After yet another stressful dinner of negotiating with Andrew to sit and eat (he resisted coming to the table or staying at the table), tensions were high. Stuart and I cleared the table, bringing plates and glasses to the kitchen. Abby was crying, sensing the strained dynamic. We promptly escorted her to her room, hoping to prevent an explosion from Andrew who was already showing signs of dysregulation, but it was too late.

From across the room, Andrew threw one of the tall, clear drinking glasses, likely an attempt to release his own stress. Still full of water, it smashed against the granite countertop, shattering into dozens of tiny fragments of glass that fell to the dark hardwood floor below. The pieces glistened.

We stood there, eyes wide, frozen. Andrew was laughing, that silly, delirious laugh, the one that drove us mad. Neither of us knew where to begin or what to do next. *Block Andrew from reentering the kitchen? Go grab a broom, a mop, a kitchen towel?* We were enraged and overwhelmed. It was like all the tension and all the dancing around to avoid this exact scenario had built up to a fiery moment where everything went up in flames and then we watched as smoke billowed and embers fell.

And then it began.

Splintered glass and spilled water still covering the floor, Stuart and I hurled hurtful comments at each other, trying to discharge all that had built up to that point. Days and weeks of tension imploded as we threw insults within those kitchen walls. I prayed that Abby was oblivious, safely in her room, unaware. She typically heard everything. I prayed she would forget most of what she heard.

Andrew had stopped laughing. Watching as his parents exploded, his crying intensified as we intensified. I imagined it wasn't so much what he saw but what he felt; he was so aware, so in tune and connected.

"This is insane! We can't live like this!" Stuart shouted.

"No one can live like this!" I retorted.

"What the hell is wrong with him! It's too much. This is crazy!"

"I know. Stu, I hear you. I don't know what to do . . . I feel like we're doing everything . . . "

"Well maybe it's too much! All the natural remedies and things we do for him. Maybe none of it's helping. Maybe we need to put him on meds . . . I don't know!"

"Ugh, I get it! What do you think, I'm not aware? That I don't wonder if any of it is helping, either? I hear you. I want things to be better too!"

"Well, they're not. Things are worse. We can't go on like this. What if we can never go out, or ever have people over again?"

I started to go quiet. I could feel myself shutting down, wondering, too, if this would be forever.

"Maybe we should live separately," I managed to shout back, and I meant it: me away from Stu, or Andrew away from both of us. "Maybe he should live with your parents . . . "

Stuart just stared at me and tersely uttered, "Maybe he should live in a home."

The words hung in the air, sharp, biting, and new. Like every word we had ever wondered but had never spoken was out now, in the open, exposed. I could feel fire rise from my chest, my cheeks flushed.

Neither of us knew what any of it meant. Were we separating? Would we actually consider having Andrew live in a group home?

We knew that for some families these were necessary options. That the demands of caring for someone with significant needs could become beyond what a household could handle.

But that's not how this felt. This felt like quitting. And although it seemed like there were limited options, and to this day Stuart will admit that he had lost all hope that night, I knew that none of it was what we wanted, either of us.

After what felt like an eternity, I mustered up the strength to look Stuart square in the face, and I declared (truthfully, on behalf of both of us):

"I will never give up on that child! Never, not ever!" My words were piercing and final.

I saw everything that had brought us to that point flash before my eyes.

Meeting Stu, getting married, announcing we were pregnant. The birth of Andrew. Our new little family. Another pregnancy, the complications, the NICU. The loss of James. The grief. Newfound hope and the birth of Abby. The future. Atypical development, the diagnosis, autism. The challenges and the hurdles. All of what we had faced and surmounted. I saw all of it: the joy, the hardship, the love.

I stopped speaking. I couldn't move. I went numb. And then I crumbled to the floor.

I never could remember what happened next, whether we cleaned up the glass or let it sit there. I can't remember if Stu stayed. I can't remember how upset Andrew was seeing my face in my hands, crying on the floor. Or if Abby ever did emerge from her room.

Everything went dark. It's all I could see.

I had nothing left. No tears, no commitment, no solutions. I felt nothing. We went to bed that night not speaking; there were no words left.

But in that moment, that awful, dark, broken evening, the answers came. They came out of the nothingness.

I wanted to quit, but I couldn't; I loved my children too much to leave them and I knew that Stuart and I were better together in this. But there was nothing more I could do. In truth, there was nothing more I *needed* to do. I was being called to surrender.

I was being called to give over all of my uncertainty, all the emptiness and fear, to something greater than myself. *What is this, this place, where there is nothing?* I wondered. I threw it all up. In that dark moment of nothing, I gave it all over: to a greater power, to my higher self, to God. I surrendered.

It was freeing. I found peace in that moment because of what occurred to me: surrender was not *giving up*–this felt more active than that. Surrender was letting go and trusting in something beyond me. Letting go of all I thought I could control, of outcomes and expectations, and trusting in the process of life. Trusting that I would be led.

Letting go was all I had.

So I did, I let go. I had nothing left *but* to let go.

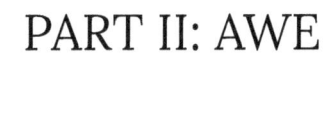

PART II: AWE

"WE'RE LEFT WITH NOTHING
BUT TO SURRENDER.
EVERYTHING ELSE
IS JUST STRUGGLE."
-ANDREW

CHAPTER 15

I let go of a lot that night, crying on the kitchen floor. More than I'd realized. I let go of the expectation that my life should look a certain way, or that my child should look a certain way—different than he was. I let go of the idea that he might change. I let it all go.

This was about finally accepting my child as he was, *because of* who he was. And finally accepting my life, *this* life, not some other version of it.

This is what it would mean to surrender to life. In doing so, I found myself open—curious, even.

What if there was something *else* out there for us? Something we didn't know about yet—a therapy or therapist. Something for me to learn? We had already done so much. And to be honest, I thought it would have looked different, looked something like this: We would continue to explore natural therapies. We'd go deeper into nutrition, do another heavy-metal cleanse and a deep metabolic reset. I'd uncover *the* natural remedy, *the missing piece*, and one day, my child would emerge; one day, it wouldn't look like autism.

Truthfully, that's what I expected. On some level, that's how I thought it *should* go—or at least what I thought was possible for my child; mine was the son of a holistic nutritionist, after all. Surely my child would be one of those children who "recovered" from autism. We had done food sensitivity testing, elimination diets, B12 injections, gut microbe testing, the GAPS diet, chelation therapy, homeopathy, metabolic testing, clay detox baths, sound therapy, cranial-sacral therapy, energy work, body work, occupational therapy, music therapy, intuitive medical readings, and psychic sessions. All these therapies and natural health protocols played a role in supporting Andrew, and yes, there was always more we *could* do. (The list of conventional and alternative therapies for autism is endless.)

But in time I would learn that autism, or Andrew, was about so much more than that—about so much more than any one thing or any one therapy, intervention, or piece to a puzzle. We would continue to do what we knew was helping: clean eating, supportive supplements, fresh air, nature, and brain–body movement therapy. Letting go meant I was no longer searching. All I had to do was be open.

I found myself happy again. I was surrendering into a life that had been created for me, and in doing so, I felt like me again. I *found* me again. I was open to life's possibilities, allowing life to reveal itself to me.

In that *dark night of the soul*, the night that stripped me of all armor, where I was left bare in my own humanness, I had to face what it meant to truly let go. Surrendering felt uncomfortable and unproductive. *Surely, I need to do more than just this?*

I didn't need to *do* anything. I just needed to be open. I just needed to be.

***

In my ongoing quest for supportive therapies for Andrew, I had found a brain–body balance method developed by a doctor in New York City. This doctor was getting great results with autistic children through identifying brain imbalances, or "functional disconnection" as he called it. His method helped mitigate the child's challenges through physical body movements, as well as nutrition and lifestyle counseling. We had seen the benefit to Andrew of brain–body movement therapy at a center in Toronto for years. Perhaps this was the next evolution of that for us. Perhaps we were headed to New York.

Something was holding me back. It could have been the money (tens of thousands on the therapy itself, let alone the cost to get there, stay there, and get back); but no, that wasn't it. It was something else. A feeling. I wasn't practiced at using my intuition, but my gut said that our next step wasn't something I'd have to plan or figure out. So, I let that go too and just remained open.

From the day I heard the term "nonverbal autism," I wondered who the people were behind the label. For years I searched for the autistic perspective, the truth of what it was like to live with autism and be autistic. I wanted to better understand. I found books written by autistic individuals and ordered them by the cartload.

I soaked up their perspectives; however, they only ever seemed to be from the view of someone who could speak and write. This wasn't our lived experience, and I was sure it wasn't Andrew's. Where were the nonspeakers? Who was speaking for them? How were their stories, their lived experiences, being shared? I didn't know where to begin looking, but I knew it didn't begin back at Andrew's diagnosis.

Andrew's diagnosis was delivered like a life sentence: apologetic, bleak, and looming. There was no guidance, no encouragement to connect with families who had gone before us, and certainly not a lot of hope for the future of children with a diagnosis of "severe nonverbal autism."

If I told you, though, that I had known there was more to Andrew than meets the eye, it would be an understatement. I could tell he knew so much. *How can we reach him?* I wondered. I yearned to truly know my child.

Or was this just how it was?

I oscillated between these realms. I wanted to live in a place of acceptance; I no longer wanted to wish for something different than who Andrew was. Except that there *was* more to him, more than what you could see by just looking. Even beyond our heart connection, it was something more tangible than that, something beyond the face of autism. I knew it. I felt it. In the moments when I would look deep into his eyes, deep until, I swear, I could see his soul, I would know. And yes, that meaningful, soulful exchange was enough, but I would always wonder.

By this point Andrew was successfully using a digital picture communication system on his iPad called Language Acquisition through Motor Planning (LAMP). He could select a string of words to form basic phrases like "I eat apple" to request an apple, or "go car" if he'd like to go for a car ride. He was able to match words to pictures of items like "iPad" or "musical toy," which was curious, as no one ever taught him how to read. He couldn't hold a pencil to write, not even his name, as his motor planning ability (the directive from his brain to his body) was so limited.

As he sat there on his device, punching out basic requests for food or a toy, proud as I was, I wondered if he was capable of more. *Is he limited by what is programmed within that app? What are his true desires? His thoughts and opinions?* Grateful for his ability to communicate with us, it still felt like such a small window into Andrew's world.

That's when all the dots began to connect.

Just like my search for the nonspeaking autistic perspective, I spent many years searching for the therapies I thought Andrew needed. Speech therapy, sensory integration therapy, behavior therapy, and movement therapy. The list went on. They all helped. His body was healthy: he ate well, he could walk, ride a bike, swim, laugh, cry, move. He could communicate through pictures. Did he need more?

Certainly, one of the most impactful forms of therapy over the years was movement therapy. A series of specific, individualized movements, practiced over weeks and months with a trained practitioner, allowed Andrew to retrace the lines of coordination in his brain. The results were apparent: he could climb the playground equipment on his own and roll successfully down a grassy hill. This was a change from his early years of disconnect apparent in his everyday functioning, with difficulty crawling, rolling, and climbing. Some days just coordinating his body in space was hard.

From the time he was little I knew brain–body therapy would be of benefit. We found a place in Toronto that offered this type of therapy. We began when Andrew was seven, traveling an hour from our home in the suburbs, and we continued right into his teenaged years after moving into the city.

Through movement therapy, Andrew carried himself differently. He became more deliberate, more *purposeful*, in his actions. His sensory system appeared more integrated. He became more focused, centered, and grounded. We expected this would benefit Andrew for years to come.

What I *didn't* expect was that it would lead us to one of the most profound, influential turn of events of our family's life.

I wasn't looking; I was being led.

"WHAT HAVE WE
GOT TO LOSE?"
–STUART

CHAPTER 16

It was spring. I was feeling resolved in my new practice of surrender. I would remind myself, again and again, that surrender wasn't giving up. I was creating space to allow for life to present itself. In letting go of what I thought life *should* look like, I could be open to life's possibilities.

At our next movement therapy session, I shared with Stephanie, the director of Andrew's programming, how I had come to this place of needing to surrender. She listened as I went through the various therapies we had used and about how confused I felt that nothing in particular had had a monumental impact on Andrew's functioning the way I expected it would. I knew that it had all helped (it had *all* made a difference), but I was no longer searching for "the magic bullet."

We watched as Andrew darted around the indoor therapy space, gym mats and wooden benches set up strategically along the thin-planked pine wooden floors. He loved it there. He was engaged, even when he struggled during a session.

I knew that Andrew was redefining my version of "normal." What did it mean to accept my child "as he was"? Was that defeatist? Was different "bad"? Was Andrew supposed to look and act like everyone else? Is that what "improvement" would look like? Who defined these norms? Society? Experts? Or parents? Could I lean into my feeling that our children were showing us a different way of being? Showing us how to fully step into ourselves?

Stephanie smiled, and in her objective, matter-of-fact way, she said, "You might be interested in a mini-documentary our center produced. It's about a boy very similar to Andrew, a few years older. We documented his progress through our therapy, but more so, I'm thinking you might connect with their story. Their family has pursued a similar approach to yours, looking at diet and nature and the brain–body connection to health. You're reminding me of them. I can send it to you, if you like."

Seven years later, I grin as I write this. It's like rewatching a scene in my life, only I know exactly what happens next. I know how the story unfolds, the divinely orchestrated sequence of events, leading from one scene to the next.

Accepting my child's autism diagnosis meant that I could be open to therapies that might help him early on. Honoring my belief and understanding of the brain–body connection meant that I could find therapists who shared similar philosophies on how to support autistic children rather than fix them. Trusting my intuition meant I could take the steps that were presenting before me.

The twenty-six-minute documentary took me an hour to watch. I paused it, jaw-dropped, countless times. I texted Stu right away: *You're going to need to watch this.* I was in tears.

The film was about a thirteen-year-old boy named Jordyn and his experience with movement and body regulation. What I marveled at was that Jordyn was using a letterboard to communicate with his mother, Kelli. So moved was I not only by the fact that this nonspeaking autistic boy was able to communicate his thoughts but also by the depth of his insight. In fact, I was humbled.

All I could see was Andrew.

For ages I wondered what the nonspeaking autistic experience truly was. I sought out books (but couldn't find them), parents (where were they?), or even practitioners who worked with nonspeakers (different from those who used a conventional approach) in order to truly understand my own child.

Can this be Andrew? Can Andrew have this level of insight and awareness? Can he, too, desire to have his thoughts known? Can he learn to use a letterboard? What is this tool? How have I never heard of it?

As parents, we speak for our children. I had spoken for Andrew since the day he was born. Advocated for him, yes, but it went beyond that. I thought for him. Imagined for him. Wished for him. I anticipated his needs and wants, his feelings and behaviors.

To watch Jordyn share the inner perspectives of *his* world and his role in *our* world was astounding, breathtaking. He doesn't speak; he spells to communicate. I was in awe. More than that, I felt encouraged. It was like watching everything I had imagined about autism, or Andrew, come to life. Up until that point, it had only been an assumption, a feeling. Now, before me, there was evidence of the true potential of my child.

I reached out to Kelli, Jordyn's mother, right away. Tongue-tied, I had question upon question, overwhelmed with what this was, and whether it would work with my child, and was it for real, and how could we get started. I asked her to please let Jordyn know how inspiring he was.

After years of digging, I had found the community of experts from whom I had longed to learn. Nonspeaking authors, advocates, students, allies and friends, this was a community of nonspeakers who had found a means to communicate *for themselves* (not the organizations that claimed to know them, represent them, or worse, speak for them).

This is when the answers came. Years of asking questions culminated in this single, life-changing moment in time. The day we abandoned conventional thinking and started believing in possibilities. The day we presumed competence above all else. The day I lessened my grip on controlling what was in order to allow for what could be.

Through the process of surrender, I had become open. And it was only from this open place that the letterboard could appear. It wasn't anything I had searched for; I had been led.

***

I should have known, based on Andrew's sounds and excitement, that we were onto something. It was November, and although the days were getting shorter, this day was bright. Andrew, Stuart, and I were headed into a studio space in Toronto that was hosting a weekend intensive for families training on the Spelling to Communicate (S2C) method. We were there to meet with the founder of the method, Elizabeth Vosseller, that sunny Friday afternoon.

We had signed up for this weekend based on a leap of faith and a glimmer of hope. I had questions and doubts. It was Stuart who said quite frankly, "What have we got to lose?"

The founder, a trained speech and language pathologist from Virginia in the United States, had traveled to Toronto as part of her mission of bringing S2C to families across the globe. She traveled the world, teaching families and training practitioners on this groundbreaking method of communication. Her stop in Toronto was completely booked, save for one opening, for one new family. Us.

It was like nothing I had ever seen before. Families across Ontario had driven in for the opportunity to train with Elizabeth. Nonspeaking autistic individuals, mostly in their teens and twenties, were waiting with their families for their scheduled session. They were flapping, jumping, and rocking in what appeared to be excitement at this opportunity. Similar communication methods, those based on the foundational understanding that being nonspeaking is not indicative of a cognitive impairment, had gone before this; however, S2C brought a systematic approach to teaching the skills required to spell on a letterboard, along with implementation strategies for families to practice on their own. Families were making all the necessary arrangements to be there.

We sat with Elizabeth, this near perfect stranger, who looked at Andrew, told him she knew he was smart, and that she would help him show the world. After reading a passage on a specific topic, she held up a large alphabet letterboard, the size of a standard piece of paper, and asked him a question. Then, she taught him how to use the letterboard through a series of prompts, engaging with Andrew in a way that honored his whole being: his personality, his need to move, and his intelligence. She showed us that Andrew could spell.

The concept of "spelling to communicate," in my mind, assumed one knew how to spell, when one had never been taught how to spell, when one had never had the ability to write. And it assumed this of Andrew. No one had taught him this. We had never sat with him and taught him the alphabet in order to put words together. We had never taught him to read. We didn't do these things because we never knew what he was capable of. Yes, we believed there was so much going on inside his mind, but he had no way of showing us—until then.

This language and communication professional changed our entire understanding of nonspeaking autism through a tool we had known nothing about: the letterboard method of communication. Elizabeth taught us that most nonspeaking autistic individuals struggle with speech for the same reason that they struggle initiating tasks or coordinating their bodies to complete an activity: there is a brain–body disconnect that originates in the brain's motor cortex. This affects motor planning (the brain's ability to tell the body what to do) and execution, or "output," but has nothing to do with cognitive ability, comprehension, or the capacity to learn. It explained why Andrew could never do sign language, write with a pencil, or speak.

Our minds were blown. If I believed that the autistic brain functioned differently, which I had seen with Andrew, surely I could entertain that Andrew might also learn in a different way? Clearly, nonspeaking did not mean nonthinking. This was a complete paradigm shift.

That weekend I watched a nonspeaking autistic teenager (who appeared completely unaware of any of us) write about courage—in between flapping his hands, rocking, and humming. Courage! I watched my own son spell "brain" after being asked what part of his body felt disconnected from him. And then "arachnid" when asked about a spider. (Stu and I laughed amid tears in our eyes—did we even know how to spell arachnid?) He spelled "Einstein" when asked about the theory of relativity. The look on Andrew's face? Unmistakable pride. Someone finally knew that *he was in there.*

We hadn't taught Andrew these words. He had never learned spelling in school. But somehow, he had been taking it all in. Maybe it was by flipping through books and magazines (including

National Geographic) long before he could walk. Maybe he was reading signs. Maybe one day we would find out.

This was exciting on so many levels. This moment in our family's life became about fortitude and belief, belief in what we couldn't see but knew to be there. It was a huge reminder to believe in possibilities. It became about trusting ourselves and abandoning convention. Clearly, though, I had been doing it all along:

When Andrew was nine months old and wasn't crawling properly, I started "cross crawl" leg and arm exercises with him, even though people laughed, having researched how important cross-lateral brain–body movement was for early development and learning. This led us to movement therapy, which, of course, led us to Jordyn and the letterboard.

When a speech pathologist told me that Andrew would likely never speak, or ever exchange meaningful conversation, and I sat in our car, bawled, then swore I would never let anyone reduce my child to such a low level of potential, ever.

When, even before a diagnosis was given, a behavior therapist laughed at me after I said, "He has always loved books. I don't know . . . maybe he can read . . . " and I vowed I would never abandon opportunities for my child to learn.

When going on instinct, I contacted Jordyn's mom just to tell her how inspired I was by what her boy was able to share, and this was when she suggested Spelling to Communicate for Andrew and let us know there was one spot left in the Toronto S2C intensive weekend. And I had said yes.

To canceling a nutrition speaking tour and saying no to a girls' weekend away, all in order to attend a weekend-long S2C training course with Stuart that would completely change the direction of our life.

To showing up, even with all the doubt and insecurity we had.

We opened a new chapter that weekend, one that, quite literally, Andrew would write.

It was hard to explain, in the days that followed, what exactly this was and what we got out of it. We were nervous, apprehensive, to say too much. Was it wishful thinking? Was it real? Could this really happen for Andrew and for us?

We told Abby.

"Abby! Guess what? We met a family today with a boy who is just like Andrew!"

"He has curly hair?" Abby cheerfully replied.

I laughed. My lovely, sincere little girl. "No, he doesn't have curly hair, actually. It's that he doesn't talk, just like Andrew. He has learned to use the letterboard, too, and just wrote a book about it."

"Oh, cool!" She nodded. She reminds me of how simple love can be. When all you've known is a brother who doesn't speak, you learn to love no matter what. Everything else is bonus.

I would never sensationalize it, but I had a feeling that this method was going to change everything.

***

The act of spelling to communicate is something that, ironically, is hard to put into words. Family, friends, readers of *Life, Love & Autism*, regularly ask us to explain it. "So, does he type on a keyboard? What do you mean, an alphabet board? He points to letters, how? Why does he need a partner with him?" It is a simple yet rigorous, fascinating, and foundational system of communication. It is one of the most misunderstood yet revolutionary methods of expression for individuals with speech challenges.

One organization, the International Association for Spelling as Communication, has championed the mission of education and advocacy for this method and for the community of people who stand to benefit.

Our family was trained specifically through the system of communication called Spelling to Communicate.

Spelling to Communicate (S2C) is a method of communication that teaches nonspeaking individuals, or individuals who have unreliable or minimal speech, to use purposeful motor skills to point to letters on a physical letterboard to communicate their thoughts, needs, and opinions. It is a form of Alternative and Augmentative Communication (AAC) and provides a reliable, effective, and robust means of communication for its user, according to the International Association for Spelling as Communication (I-ASC).

The type of letterboard used is decided (based on the individual's needs and progression) by a certified S2C practitioner who is rigorously trained by I-ASC. The letterboard is held for the "speller" by a communication and regulation partner (CRP) (a trusted person in the individual's life, often a parent or caregiver, friend or worker, who has been trained by a certified S2C practitioner), while the speller points to letters on the letterboard. The CRP supports the speller in developing the necessary skills, accuracy, and fluency to communicate.

According to I-ASC, the S2C method is based on the presumption that all individuals can and do want to learn; therefore, S2C uses age-appropriate lessons while practicing the purposeful motor skills of pointing to individual letters and sequences of letters. The lessons keep the speller cognitively engaged while they practice the motor movements necessary for communication, while also strengthening the respect and trust between speller and CRP. Because fine motor coordination can be challenging for those with motor difficulties, S2C utilizes the gross motor movement of the arm, making initiating and pointing to letters more accessible. (For most people, communication typically occurs through the fine motor movements of articulators—vocal organs—and fingers.) The goal is to achieve synchrony between the brain and body for the purpose of meaningful communication for each individual. www.i-asc.org

Spelling to Communicate is not as simple as it may seem. It became clear to me that it would take hours and hours of practice with Andrew to reach fluency on the letterboard. Not only did I need to learn how to prompt Andrew through progressing on the boards, but I would also need to help him regulate his body enough to do so. (And his was a busy body!) But I was in. Words would lead to sentences that would lead to opening up a whole new world of expression, communication, and possibility for my child.

This was different to how Andrew used his iPad to communicate, using pictures and symbols with words. Andrew was limited to whatever vocabulary had been programmed (deemed important or useful by the app developers, consulting professionals, and sometimes, by us, his parents) into the communication app, but not necessarily based on what Andrew desired to say.

Most people are curious if Andrew might eventually use the keyboard screen on his iPad to communicate with words. Perhaps. However, there is limited tactile feedback for Andrew when he touches his screen. As well, he still requires a regulation partner to aid in attending to the letterboard, someone he can trust with his words. There seems to be a societal fixation on technology that it is perhaps somehow more efficient, more independent, and more successful for a nonspeaker like Andrew. There are many nonspeakers fluent in independent typing who still prefer the traditional "physical" letterboard method to communicate. It will be up to Andrew to decide.

In many ways, there was so much at stake. This new method of communication, and the testimony of other spellers who had gone before us, offered us the chance to truly get to know Andrew. I wanted it to work, *badly*.

One night, not long into the method, I broke. I had been working at accepting my child for nearly a decade, learning to truly love him for who he was—with or without words. On some level, though, my desire to connect more deeply with Andrew remained. The potential of this method had brought that possibility even closer.

"Andrew, I just feel so grateful that we found this method, that we will finally get to know you, finally hear your voice." He came and sat with me. That's when my tears came.

The tears were for everything. For the overflowing gratitude I felt that this method had found us. For all the years of guessing, all the difficultly, all the exhaustion. For the sadness in having thought we might not ever unlock our child. And for Andrew, for his tenacity, for sticking with this life, knowing that no one knew just how smart he was.

Andrew looked at me. He looked at me with his deep brown eyes, like he always had, but it was different. Because it *was* different now; he knew that *we knew* now too.

Andrew and I sat and practiced with the boards every night. We would go down to the basement after dinner, to a little table where we had two chairs set up: one swivel, so that Andrew could spin when he needed some sensory input, and one for me, specifically for letterboard practice.

Most nights he willingly came down. It had become a ritual; he had learned to expect it. On some level, I think he knew it was his way out, his path to freedom. I would bring his favorite snacks down so he could crunch to focus, another piece of sensory input that would help him regulate, help him attend. On the table was a notebook, a few pencils, and the letterboards. There, we read books or went through topic lessons that prompted Andrew to spell different words in order to fine-tune the physical act (or motor path) of pointing to letters, essentially, to spell to communicate. There was a systematic method and I was determined to follow it. So much of it was based on consistency and trust, which I knew. I was ready to offer both.

Stuart was keen to learn too, but we were advised that it was best to start with one new partner at a time. The very first CRP relationship would establish the foundation for most of the partnerships to come. Because I spent more time with Andrew, we decided I would take it on. Passionate and committed, I was ready.

Clearly, I wanted it to be successful. What I needed to learn was that this would take whatever time it needed to take. Each individual trajectory was different. Andrew would reach fluency in his own timing. Our partnership would strengthen and develop over time. I would have to let go of any expectation of timeline for acquisition of the motor skills and for our partnership.

So attached to the outcome was I that I unknowingly put pressure on myself and on Andrew to learn the method and become "open" (being *open* meant being able to answer subjective, "open-ended" questions) as soon as possible. Even after weeks and months of progress, I was comparing Andrew to other spellers who had become fluent in a shorter period of time.

It peaked one night when I threw the boards across the room and shouted, "Andrew! We need this to work! This method–these words–this is your everything!" I was sweating, flushed by frustration and guilt. Frustrated by how tedious and ungratifying the early days of letterboard training and practice felt. Guilt at having any expectation of my child, and of myself, beyond what we were capable of, at that moment in time.

We needed to take a break. This became important—to take breaks—not just within each practice session but breaks from learning the method itself. We would pause for a week, sometimes two. When we resumed, it was with a fresh perspective.

With a bit of coaching and mentorship from the letterboard practitioner and parent community, I softened into the process. I relaxed into the belief that my child would get it in his own right timing. In turn, Andrew's trust in me was reestablished.

Even with all the hope and commitment I put into this method, and all the practice I was prepared to do, I promised myself that I would still love Andrew *without* these words. That Andrew's life was meaningful and purposeful regardless, and that our love and connection as a family was *beyond* words. There is inherent value in life just by being alive, being human, being born—with or without the ability to use words, spoken or written.

Still, we forged ahead with the hope that giving Andrew this tool for communication would give *him* an opportunity to truly be heard.

"I WANT THE WORLD TO KNOW
THAT WE ARE WHOLE,
NOT BROKEN."

-ANDREW

CHAPTER 17

It would be one year before Andrew shared anything open with me on the letterboard. Up to that point, our dialogue included knowledge-based, closed-ended questions and answers within the S2C lesson. We were continuing to practice most nights and had come to a productive structure and flow in our sessions.

Knowing Andrew needed frequent movement breaks to keep his body regulated and attentive enough to sit and spell with me, I would read through a topic of interest (from a book or article I had sourced), one paragraph at a time, inserting a necessary body break in between. At the end of each paragraph, I would ask Andrew to come back, sit, and spell a few key "known" words (or "spell words") with me. (*Spell words* were words I had spelled aloud while I was reading from the text. *Spell words* were a simple way to practice the motor actions of getting to the correct or intended letter.) Andrew would point, letter by letter, to spell out the word. Over time, he required less and less of the S2C prompts to spell with accuracy. As well, I would ask him one or two specific questions related to the material I had just read aloud. Even though his body would be busy running around, his mind was actively taking it all in. He would sit in the swivel chair beside me, weighted down with heavy sandbags that I placed on his lap to help regulate his body, snacking on pieces of celery, and with his finger up and ready to point, he would spell out the correct answer. He would prove it to me every time.

The shift we saw in Andrew was beyond obvious. Since this new method of communication, he carried himself with a sense of pride and a knowing; people knew now that he was smart. We saw fewer meltdowns, fewer tears. He was more engaged and would spend more time lingering around (as we called it). I continued to be amazed by the whole process. Here we were, defying conventional autism norms, proving that not being able to speak was not the same as not having something to say.

And one day it "clicked."

It was just before Halloween. Knowing how bizarre a tradition this holiday was for Andrew (with years of him crying in costumes he didn't want to wear, throwing himself on the steps of houses he didn't want to approach, and having no interest in collecting or eating candy), I pulled up any and all resources I could use to explain it, including the tradition of All Saints' and All Souls' Day. I found a letterboard lesson on The Day of the Dead, the Mexican tradition that is a blend of traditions from Aztec Mesoamerica and Catholicism.

We began with spelling out some *spell words*, then we went through a few specific questions, all of which he answered correctly. I looked at him, curious, and then asked, spontaneously:

"Can you name one other religion?"

And he spelled out: HINDUISM. I was shocked. *How in the world does this child know about Hinduism?* And how timely: it was the celebration of Hinduism's largest holiday that week. *Does he know that too?* I wondered, so, I asked:

"What holiday are Hindus celebrating tomorrow?"

D I V A L I, he pointed out, letter by letter.

I pushed it further:

"And Divali can be spelled with a 'v' or with which other letter?"

And, very confidently, he pointed to the W.

I was astounded.

As awful as it was to admit, we were only just beginning to appreciate that Andrew had been aware of so much more than just his surroundings. Before this, we had no real idea what he knew, to what extent, if at all. (And clearly, he also had some grasp on cultural traditions!) What else did he know? What else could we find out? What is it that he might want to tell us?

I grabbed Andrew by the arms. "Andrew! This is incredible! Can you believe it? Oh my goodness, there is so much ahead. I can just feel it."

He looked at me like "Of course I can believe it. This is me. I've always been here."

It was a moment I will never forget. I knew from that point forward there was no turning back.

Imagine finally getting to know your child, like *really* getting to know them. Ten years and you finally access the person you knew existed but that you couldn't reach—the bright mind and beautiful soul you saw in their eyes. Not deficient. Not less. Just somehow out of reach.

Imagine the look in *your child's eyes* when they know you're finally seeing them.

Imagine, for the first time, your child being able to put a feeling, an explanation, to something. Something you knew existed beyond the pictorial system you've prompted him to use. Imagine finally being able to express your thoughts, your perspectives, your opinions. No one speaking for you. Your own words. Your authentic voice.

Imagine me, his mother, loving him all these years because he is mine, even when it was hard and I wanted to quit. Imagine, then, sitting down with him to do a lesson on holidays, and when asked which holiday he enjoys most, he spells out C H R I S T M A S . And your heart melts and your eyes well with tears and you cry out with excitement and pride, "Andrew! That is so amazing! Good for you, bud!" as he spells it out, letter by letter, and he looks at you, coy, like "Yah, that's right. I'm here. You know I'm here."

I used to cry a lot. Sometimes my tears would come out of helplessness. I would look at Andrew and know that he was *in there* but not know how to get him out, or if it was even possible. No one talks about letterboard communication in conventional autism therapy; we doubt its potential, just like we doubt our children.

But imagine how this new tool would change everything with your child: your experience with them, your interactions with them, your appreciation of them. Because it has—it has changed everything.

It had been ten years of life with Andrew. In ten years and no spoken conversations, I knew this child just as much as I knew his sister. You get to know the subtleties of your child, things you miss in the words and noise of regular life with regular kids.

The letterboard changed things for our family in a way that's almost embarrassing to admit. It changed the way we spoke to Andrew and about Andrew. We include him now in conversations where before he might have been overlooked. We might have thought he was content "in his own world" (let alone that he might have something to say). And it changed our outlook; the future looked more inclusive and more hopeful.

It *didn't* change that autism is still hard; autism can be very hard at times. (I have important papers hidden away, and favorite plants in hard-to-reach places.) But what I know now is that this has everything to do with a brain–body disconnect, not *behavior*. Andrew often can't control how his impulsive body acts, and his brain knows differently. What we might see as "challenging behavior," we are learning, may actually be a body acting out something quite different from what the individual knows or feels inside. What might look like stress, even dysregulation, may actually be excitement—laughter or perhaps anxiety. Even facial expressions are not always reflective of the person's true state of being. Stu and I have to remind each other to no longer assume. And the only person to identify how they are truly feeling is the nonspeaking individual, Andrew.

It also didn't change that there is still *disability*. We were learning to support Andrew for his strengths *and* his challenges, seeing disability not as a bad word but as something that exists in the fabric of being human, something for all of us to accommodate, support, and embrace.

Without a doubt, the letterboard changed the way we saw life.

***

Andrew and I continued to practice on the letterboard, and Andrew continued to amaze me.

This one night was no different.

After reading about the trials of decision-making, and how sometimes you just need to trust your gut and "go for it," I asked Andrew a few questions about the lesson, using the letterboard. The book quoted Wayne Gretzky, renowned professional hockey player. I read the quote aloud to Andrew and spelled out Gretzky's name. I wasn't surprised when Andrew was able to spell back WAYNE GRETZKY.

But then I asked him something we hadn't talked about: "What sport did Gretzky play?"

And Andrew spelled out: HOCKEY

"How did you know that Wayne Gretzky played hockey?"

I READ IT.

My eyes widened. I was spellbound, smiling. This might not seem like a big deal—everyone knows Gretzky played hockey—but who told Andrew? We're not a hockey family; we don't talk about that stuff.

Sure, maybe he heard it somewhere, but Andrew himself said he read it. He (and other largely underestimated, nonspeaking individuals) has likely, literally, been observing print *his whole life*: signs, books, television. Andrew has been flipping through magazines and books since he was a baby.

This was a *huge* deal. I wanted to take it further, so I asked Andrew about the quote. "What do you think of Wayne Gretzky's words?" Andrew got upset. It was a Friday night and I imagined he might want to say "Ugh, Mom! Like, seriously? Can we take the night off?" I no longer assume. What I know now about Andrew's brain-body disconnect is that sometimes what appears on the outside is not reflective of what's actually being felt on the inside. What might look like "upset" to me might actually be excitement, anxiety, or an uncontrolled body impulse. Yes, maybe the quote was, in fact, quite meaningful, maybe too meaningful for Andrew right then, but it was only Andrew who could tell me.

"Can you tell me what you think of Gretzky's quote?" NO

"Are you all done?" A L L   D O N E   T O D A Y.

And, quite matter-of-factly, we both got up.

Of course, Gretzky's words echoed in my head: "You miss 100 percent of the shots you don't take."

All I could think was *I'm so glad we took this shot.*

***

Now, before our story continues, I must be clear:

This is not just my child. My child is not special. (I mean, yes, he is special. Of course, he's special in that he's mine, he's courageous, and he is a gift.) He's not special in that this method only worked *because it was Andrew.* This method is for everyone. It is not unique to a certain category of person. There is not a specific set of criteria to be successful. It spans no age, race, or gender limitation. It is for the child who moves constantly, or sits still, and the adult who flaps and rocks and hums, or is silent. It can be used by the minimally speaking, unreliably speaking, and nonspeaking alike. Yes, it requires the ability of an individual to move their body in such a way that they can select a letter on a board, but even formal pointing is flexible. It requires a letterboard partner to assist in helping the individual regulate such that they are able to meet the board and engage with it, but nothing more than what already exists in a trusted relationship between two people who know each other's needs.

We did not formally sit and teach Andrew how to read, or spell, or follow letters on a page. He is not unique in his ability to learn a new skill, to learn the motor process required to create output. He is unique in his thoughts, yes, his opinions and his desires. Just like all of us, there are funny people and soulful people and people who like country music and people who like nature. So it is with Andrew and other nonspeakers. Andrew is introspective; his friend, William, is comedic (although Andrew can be very funny, as can William be reflective). Nothing about this method informs the individual of who they are supposed to be; they emerge with the letterboard tool exemplifying who they are.

Spelling to Communicate requires a leap of faith and a presumption that your child, your loved one, wishes to be heard—maybe even has something to say. It requires the parent to abandon the risk that "it will be too hard"; "my child won't get it"; "this is just not for us." *What if it is? What if they do get it? What if it changes everything?*

Yes, it *is* hard, sometimes. It is hard for Andrew to put into words what he is feeling or thinking or knowing. It takes massive effort, concentration, and stamina to produce statements on the letterboard. Never do we take for granted even the smallest word, as it is still far more than we ever had access to before.

"EVERYONE IS PERFECT
FOR WHO THEY ARE."
−ABBY

CHAPTER 18

Stuart and I, and Abby, are constantly on the edge of our seat, blown away by Andrew's words and his ability to communicate. *What might he share next? What might we learn about him? How might we help make his life in this world more understandable, more forgiving, more tolerant?*

This is the power of self-advocacy and self-expression.

At the first signs of spring, we get the kids on their bikes. We ride a few streets. Nothing new. All good. One day we came home and Andrew had a huge fit, throwing his bike down, running inside, crying.

What in the world? Automatically, my mind ran the list to find the trigger. "Was he . . . ?" Hungry, hurt, tired, cold, overwhelmed? Was it too busy?

In the past, Stuart and I would sit in the frustration of it—the guessing game from which you might not ever get an answer. This time I plunked Andrew in front of the letterboard, crying fit and all (which is never a good idea, as it's hard to communicate feelings when you're so *in them*).

"What happened, Andrew? Why are you crying after the bike ride?"

It's still very hard for Andrew to coordinate his eyes-brain-hand to spell on the letterboard, but doesn't he spell out: D I D N ' T L I K E S T R E E T N O I S E. His whole body relaxed and his tears stopped.

Therein lies the power of this tool, for never in a million years could we have gotten that out of his picture communication system. Not that kind of depth or clarity. And certainly not that kind of sympathy, in truth, from us. Likely, not the same level of relief for him either. Andrew is less frustrated, more content, feels esteemed, purposeful, and impactful. He tells us this.

This child deserves so much more credit.

Can you imagine the trapped experience of someone who is nonspeaking? How excruciating it must be sometimes? And for the parent, it often ends in total frustration, anger, arguments, or despair.

The story gets better.

A few weeks later, we went out on that same bike ride. It was an awesome, really fun time. I could tell Andrew was loving it. When we got home, I asked him with the letterboard: "Did you enjoy tonight's bike ride? Yes or no?" And he spelled out: Y E S

"What did you enjoy about it?"

S P E E D - R I D I N G   W I T H   M Y   D A D. (Which is so fantastic, because that's exactly what they did.)

"How do you feel now that you can ride a bike?"

H A P P Y   A N D   P R O U D.

"What were the street sounds like tonight?"

A   L O T   Q U I E T E R   T O N I G H T.

I was curious. "Did you hear the overhead wires at the big school?" (Kind of a leading question, because I myself had heard them. I suspect he hears more than we can.)

Y E S, he confirmed.

"How would you describe their sound? Noisy? Quiet? Irritating?"

NOISY

"Is that the noisy part of the bike ride?" YES

"How did you manage it tonight?"

SOMETIMES I MANAGE.

And there it was, a conversation with my child. Something I could never have had prior to the letterboard. There would be more like these.

Like the time when Grandpa asked Andrew about the leaves. For years Andrew has listened to nature. We would watch him, when he was little, holding a pine cone up to his ear. We imagined he was listening to the sound it made in his hand, but we were only guessing. When he got older, he listened to leaves, of all different shapes and sizes, that he would hold up to his ear, flicking each one, then letting them go to move on to the next.

One day, seeing this, my dad asked:

"What do you hear, Andrew?"

Andrew spelled out on his letterboard: I HEAR THE FREQUENCY. I HEAR ALL OF THE SOUNDS THAT NATURE MAKES.

It's true. There is an actual frequency, like an "energetic blue-print," in all things. It can be soundless, but it exists.

Andrew's sense of sound has always been acute, often to the point of being unbearable. But that same "burden" has gifted him with an ability to hear that which most of us can't—and I expect it's quite magnificent.

Turns out, he listens to everything, and always has, all those years. The years when we talked over him, didn't include him, assumed things, made decisions on his behalf. He was listening. He heard it all. I am forever in awe at how he navigated his life without words—without being able to interject, defend, contribute, of self-advocate. Now he can. He writes: I NEED TO MAKE MYSELF HEARD.

Andrew's greatest challenge will continue to be his brain–body disconnect. Motor planning and execution impact his ability to carry out everyday tasks, to coordinate his body, and, of course, to speak. This was only the beginning of us learning what it felt like for Andrew to be in his body.

IT IS A HUGE DEAL TO GET MY BODY TO DO WHAT MY BRAIN WANTS IT TO DO. WHAT LOOKS LIKE DISINTEREST OR INATTENTION IS ACTUALLY AN INABILITY TO DO WHAT I WANT MY BODY TO DO. I WORK SO HARD AT THESE BODY-BRAIN TASKS. YOU WILL NEVER KNOW JUST HOW HARD IT IS.

Years later, we have confirmation of what we always suspected to be true. Absolutely remarkable.

***

The relationship between Andrew and Abby continued to grow and change. Through the letterboard, Abby was able to connect with the brother she loved in a new, more tangible way. She loved him unconditionally, but now, there were words. And *was she enamored!*

Full of ideas from newfound inspiration, Abby woke one morning, saying: "Mama! Last night I had a dream that we wrote a book about Andrew—like, he wrote it, too—we put *his* words into it—you know, what he's spelling to you—we put it into a book—so basically, it's like he was writing the book too."

Abby wakes up most mornings in full conversation mode,

ready to start the day. That morning was no exception. Full-on sometimes, but so, so honoring of her brother. Every morning she would ask, "What did Andrew spell?" She knew we practiced before bed most nights.

She continued. "And then we can tell people about it, and make photocopies of it, and sell it—like, to our neighbors. And Andrew would get paid from the books we sell. That's how he would make some money. And then Dada wouldn't have to pay Andrew into his bank account because Andrew would have his own money from the book we put together."

My lovely child. I tell her I think it's a great idea and that I've had one similar. I tell her I've had a dream of writing a book too, from about the time when our journey began—from when I started writing, documenting.

I pictured all of these little stories, our sharings, in one place. A book that parents would read, parents who were craving what I craved when we first started this journey. That period of time when you feel alone and confused. When you wish for inspiration. When you just want to connect with someone who is on a similar path. And then, of course, all the other stories, the new stories, about when the words came. Andrew's words. The book of our story. I would write it one day, I told her. I told her that I thought we could share it beyond just our neighbors.

Who would have thought. Yes, *it's a great idea, Abby.*

Abby's loyalty to her brother is steadfast, even when the outward expression of that love appears unrequited.

Writing one day for *Life, Love & Autism*, I started by saying:

```
"Well, I was going to write about something completely
different than this, but way more important words have
just been shared!"
```

I included a copy of exactly what I wrote to our family in a text just moments before:

```
Andrew just told Abby he loved her! He wrote it with his
letters. It was the most beautiful thing. I am crying,
Abby is crying. She is feeling tears of joy for the first
time, age seven.
```

Truth is, his words came from a burst of anger.

Sitting down to eat across from his sister, Andrew got upset. We think sometimes even the sight of her can make him angry. We've never known why and it's hard for everyone. Tired of guessing, I got out the letterboard.

Hand shaking, then calm, Andrew pointed to the letters: I AM SEARCHING FOR MY WORDS.

Imagine if we all took a moment to collect our words before we spoke!

He continued: ABBY IS PERFECT AND I AM NOT. I AM LIMITED IN MY ABILITIES. I WISH I WAS A NORMAL CHILD.

This child! That statement. Those words. It took everything for him to share: breathing with him, encouraging him to continue, plus his own tenacity and determination to finish. How insightful. How honest. How brave.

Abby and I were stunned. Tongue-tied, we didn't quite know what to say. We spilled out words of love, of how amazing we thought he was, of how we all have challenges and strengths.

Abby told him that she loved him exactly as he was, that no one was perfect, but actually, that "everyone is perfect for who they are," she said. "You're my best brother."

I asked Andrew if he wanted to reply. He raised his arm, pointed with his finger, and spelled: ABBY IS LOVING TO ME.

"And what would you like to say to her, Andrew?"

I LOVE YOU, ABBY, VERY MUCH.

And that's when the tears came. Abby, me, all of us.

Spellbound, Abby said, "I've never heard those words before." Her words hung in the air, delicate and truthful. To see my seven-year-old, Abby, experience tears of joy was one of the most beautiful, most pure expressions of love I had ever witnessed.

She gathered herself and continued. "Wow, that just made my day! And you know what, Andrew? I love you too."

I'm bawling, moved beyond words.

Abby and I danced around for the rest of the night. There were more hugs. But there was still some anger from Andrew, I could tell.

He wrote: MY EMOTIONS ARE NOT ME. He still felt angry that Abby could speak and not him. It ended with me asking Andrew what we could do about it.

"Would you like Abby to learn to use the letterboard with you?"

YES, he wrote. Abby beamed.

"Do you think Abby knows, enough, how to spell?"

NO, BUT SHE WILL LEARN. And we all laughed. It was one of those moments where I pinched myself, asking: *Is this my life?*

***

My experience of motherhood was changing, evolving. There was a joy—a lightness—I hadn't known for a little while but was familiar. It was always there; I was just seeing it through a different set of lenses now. Surrender was allowing me to enjoy what was in front of me. I had worked hard at letting go of what I couldn't control, like people's moods or our progress on the letterboard. And I embodied more of the life I was meant to live each day. I could savor the present moment and reflect on just how awesome it truly was.

"JOY JUST IS."

–ANDREW

CHAPTER 19

The summer after we launched into Spelling to Communicate, we experienced one of the most poignant periods of growth in our family's life. Five years—even one year—prior, I hadn't thought anything like it was possible; it was more a dream, something I'd have to "see to believe." And yet there it was, right in front of us.

Andrew and I flew to Virginia, USA, to attend a weekend conference for nonspeakers. The fact that there was *a conference for nonspeakers, attended by nonspeakers*, blew my mind to begin with! The privilege of it all; it was like nothing I could have imagined. Parents, practitioners, communication advocates, and nonspeakers alike. Witnessing these self-advocates "spell to communicate," sharing their thoughts, their opinions, their absolute *expertise* on the lived experience of being a nonspeaking autistic person . . . what we experienced was, ironically, hard to put into words.

To meet the father of a thirteen-year-old girl, brand new to this method of communication, who asked his daughter what she wanted to study, now that she could finally output her thoughts, and she spelled out "Math, because it's so ridiculously easy," to the awe of her parents.

To be inspired by the words of a nonspeaking university undergrad named Samuel: "Rebel against low expectations," commanding us to never settle for less.

To the countless messages Andrew received from his fellow nonspeaking peers:

"Awesome to have you here, Andrew!"

"So great you're learning this method. It'll change your life."

"Andrew and Susan, keep going. There's so much ahead."

And to see Andrew, the look of pride on his face knowing these were his people. Still at the beginning of his letterboard journey, Andrew mostly watched as his peers spelled with each other, made jokes, and shared insight and opinions. It took focus, deep processing and self-regulation for Andrew to be there. And I got to observe it all. It was a most memorable week.

Then, we traveled by car to Quebec, Canada, for a week of adventure, canoeing, hiking, and hanging out—even dropping in on friends. Throw in a 12 km family bike ride! All of it felt momentous. It required flexibility and resilience, something our family had struggled with up to that point.

To see your daughter take her older brother's hand while announcing they're "a team" at the start of your first big family hike. (You look at their dad, surprised, like *Is this really happening?*)

To sit at a restaurant, as a family, and finish a meal. (As Stuart said, "Might I actually order another beer?") No meltdowns. No tears. With photos, smiles, and silent disbelief that this is your life.

Watching Andrew transition from the plane ride home after the conference to packing up the car for a road trip to Quebec, with all of the new pieces of adventure included, was like watching a beautiful glass vase teeter on the edge of a shelf that is your life: holding your breath knowing that if it falls, it will smash into a thousand tiny pieces on the floor. (And it will be you picking up the pieces and putting them back together.) But then watching as it steadies itself, balancing itself right there on the shelf—in all of its beauty and fragility—all on its own. And you want to grab it and kiss it, gushing with pride and almost humble admiration for all of its fortitude and inner conviction to exist. To stand upright, intact, present, and spectacular. And you marvel at its presence in your life.

To the possibility of life: We never truly know what lies ahead.

To being open.

To dreaming and believing.

***

One night, over a year into the method, I told Andrew that he'd be visited at the autism center by the Toronto school board. I told him that we were hoping he could attend "Abby's school," that we'd had a positive, open conversation with the principal about how smart Andrew was. And how, with the right support, we thought it would be an important opportunity for inclusion—for Andrew and for all the students.

We were practicing on the letterboard when I said to Andrew, "Andrew, tomorrow you're going to be visited by the school board 'special services' team. They want to meet you and see what you're up to, you know, because we know how smart you are. We're hoping you will go to Abby's school—maybe just a few days a week—so that you're part of the community, and so that you can learn with your same-age peers. We'll just see how it goes, right? Try it out? Do you think it's a good idea, Andrew? Yes or no?" (We use yes/no questions on the letterboard versus open-ended questions with Andrew when we want to elicit a clear, distinct answer, at this stage.)

But Andrew didn't point to the Y or the N. He hovered around the S.

"Come on, Andrew. Go. Yes this is a good idea to try out Abby's school, or no?"

He kept pointing to the S. So I went with it.

"S, what, Andrew? S . . . "

S C H O O L . Doesn't he spell out *school*.

"Okay, school. Keep going." I was trying to hold back my elated curiosity so I could be an effective, not dysregulated, communication partner for Andrew.

Painstakingly, letter by letter, he continued: I S M Y D R E A M .

I choked up, tears streaming down my face.

"Wow, Andrew! Oh my goodness, good for you! That's amazing! Okay, well, do you think the visit will be exciting, stressful, overwhelming?" I tried to remain calm. I was jumping out of my skin.

He spelled: N O T S T R E S S F U L .

"Okay. Well, how will you be when the school people come? Excited? Silly? Anxious?"

M Y S E L F . And he got up and kissed the back of my head. Of course, I was bawling. Ten years of wondering who this child was. Ten years as his mother and I was *hearing*, for the very first time, his own independent thoughts; I was seeing them in front of my eyes.

He's just so beautiful. *Of course you will be yourself, my sweet Andrew.*

I kept thinking: *Is this happening? Is this really happening?*

Only a year prior we noticed regressive behavior whenever Andrew attended the autism center—still making gains but exhibiting behavior that, to a tuned-in parent, looked like a child who was bored. A child on repeat. He later confirmed (using his letterboard) that he was, in fact, "bored silly."

When we knew there was so much more to Andrew, we knew we had to start looking at options, options to give him access to learning, knowledge, and appropriate, relevant, age-level stimulation and engagement.

So, the research began. Private schools. "Special" schools. And regular school. Tons of advocacy, analysis, and gut feelings. Our instincts prevailed. We started Andrew at "Abby's school," our local school, in a regular class full of exceptionally kind kids. We made it happen. It was our next step, though nothing is forever, we were learning. We would be constantly revisiting where and how Andrew spent his time.

We started with a classroom introduction. All eyes on Andrew. Hearts on our sleeves. We had prepared a short paragraph on who Andrew was, explaining this new letterboard tool, and of how we hoped he would be included in their classroom. After, we asked Andrew about it:

"Did you enjoy meeting the grade fives?"

YES

"How did you feel meeting them? What emotion: happy, sad, anxious, excited?"

VERY NERVOUS TO MEET THEM.

"So why do you want to go, Andrew?"

TO LEARN.

This kid. Of course he wanted to learn! So we moved forward. Step by step, day by day. That's all you can ever really do anyway. He wouldn't have his letterboard with him at school as no one in the school (or school board, for that matter) had used the letterboard with a student like Andrew before. No one had been trained. We wanted Andrew to be included, regardless. We had no idea that this was like sending a blind child to school without their white cane.

Days before his official first day, I chatted with Andrew about how long he'd be there (just the morning); that he'd be with a support person (an educational assistant—EA); and that he wouldn't be using his letterboard at school yet, but would he like to share a message in advance with the grade 5 class?

He spelled out: LOOKING FORWARD TO LEARNING WITH YOU.

Over the weeks that followed, I was blown away not only by the words that Andrew continued to share through the letterboard but also by his overall disposition, including when I picked him up from school: content, pleased, and a little relieved. He told me he had felt overwhelmed. When I asked him how he would work at feeling less overwhelmed, he wrote: PRACTICE BEING THERE. *Of course, Andrew. So wise.*

"Andrew, do you know the goal your dad and I have for you, with being at school?"

EXPOSURE TO GREAT LEARNING. Me, dumb-founded and in awe again.

"What is it like to be in a classroom with your peers, learning?" I asked curiously.

AMAZING

My heart.

I brought the letterboard in to show Andrew's EA. I had talked about it, but Andrew and I had never demonstrated it at school publicly. Andrew's principal and EA both knew there was training involved in using the method; not just anyone could pick up the letterboard and start communicating with Andrew, which is why I never sent the letterboard in with Andrew to school.

It was the end of the morning. I knew I was pushing my luck, but I asked, "Andrew, are you okay if we show Mr. A how you do your spelling?"

YES

I took a deep breath. This somehow meant a lot, maybe mostly to me. Right there, in the open space of the school foyer, in front of his EA (and a few random kids who were around), I lifted the letterboard and we *heard* from Andrew.

"Did you enjoy your morning today, Andrew?"

YES, he replied, in front of everyone, on the spot, in a different environment than we were used to. I was in awe. We were on our way, publicly spelling in front of others!

"What was one thing you enjoyed?"

BEING OUTSIDE. I laughed. *Of course.* Being outside was Andrew's medicine.

A few other questions (and answers), and then one final question:

"What is your message for Mr. A?" Mr. A was Andrew's EA and his demeanor was much like Andrew's: quiet, soft-spoken, observant. I expected Andrew might have something to say to him.

I held my breath. This could go anywhere. Andrew could get upset. He could refuse to spell. He could write something truthful—positive *or* negative. We all watched as Andrew spelled out, letter by letter:

YOU ARE AWE . . . (the EA and I began to smile) S O M E.

Right in front of our eyes, in front of everyone to see. This was a big deal, a huge feat for Andrew. It required concentration and focus to be able to track the letters, while pointing, while managing any distractions in the background. To have others watching, well, it would be a lot for any of us! I was so proud. Again, *pinch me*, I thought. *I'm not making this up! I'm not telling him what to spell. I'm not moving the board or making him do it. This is all Andrew. This is really happening.*

Andrew's ability to self-express and self-advocate would be one of the greatest gifts to come out of Spelling to Communicate. I know Andrew is just as thankful as we are that we trusted our gut and took this next step.

***

As the following school year approached, I asked Andrew, "Do you still want to go to school?" He had been saying, through the summer, that he was keen.

YES

"Why?" I asked him, curious.

And, quite deliberately, he responded, word for word: P E O P L E NEED TO KNOW THAT I AM SMART.

My heart stopped. I could only imagine what it has been like to be Andrew. All those years, people (including his own family) never truly knowing just how smart he was. Or what he was capable of. Or how much he has, perhaps, wanted to share.

I continued: "What are you hoping to gain?"

MORE KNOWLEDGE.

On that official first day of school for Andrew, he walked in like he'd been met with something familiar, something important, something of such value to him.

"How did that go for you, Andrew?" I asked him, holding my breath, when I came to pick him up. (I was always holding my breath, it seemed! I wondered if there would ever come a day when I wouldn't hang on the edge of what Andrew was about to write.)

Methodically, Andrew spelled out: I AM SO HAPPY TO BE A PART OF THIS SCHOOL.

My dearest Andrew, I thought as I hugged him. *I wish you every single piece of knowledge you crave. Every single thing that your mind and heart desires. For you are far more deserving of this than me, than most of us. To watching your journey unfold, my child.*

It wasn't long before I realized the obvious: My children attended the same school. *The same school!* This was a first. They would share the same assemblies and the same spirit days with the same kids from the same neighborhood, the ones who would all benefit from having Andrew there. The more we can spend time with diversity in our classrooms, the more we will see acceptance, compassion, and inclusion in our children and our communities.

Every time I heard Abby say, "I saw Andrew at school today," my heart would swell a little more. It's a big deal for her too. Before Andrew started at *her* school, I asked her how she felt. I wondered if she might feel embarrassed; Andrew makes unique sounds, can be very vocal, and is clearly a student with "extra needs." She quietly confided that she was worried about Andrew attending. Worried, not embarrassed. "They don't go in pairs to the bathroom when you're in grade six, Mom. Andrew won't know how to go by himself." She's so caring, so aware. "Oh, Abby. You're so good to think of that. Andrew will have someone with him, helping him, who can show him where to go. There is probably a single bathroom that he can use, especially if he needs help." She was relieved. A smile crept across her face.

"It's Toronto Raptors Day tomorrow, Mom. We'll both have to wear red." She said, proudly, "Andrew, I'll help you pick out what you should wear" like the big little sister she is.

Moments like this made it worth the advocacy and effort required. It was only two mornings, at this point, and it was *only* because we'd created a flexible work-life for me. But so *far*, *so good*. I saw the benefit all over Andrew's face.

One week, on a typical busy school morning of breakfast dishes and lunch prep, Andrew took me by the hand and pointed to "sit" in his picture communication app. So, I sat. And it just seemed like Andrew had something to say. I held up his letterboard (which sits out now, as it should).

"How are you?" I asked.

He spelled out: I AM HAPPY I AM GOING TO SCHOOL.

Curious, I asked him, "How is school different from the autism center?"

And without hesitation, he wrote, I FEEL LIKE A NORMAL KID.

My heart expanded. I choked up. *No doubt, Andrew, I bet. Of course you do.*

I looked at him, beaming. "I'm so proud of you, Andrew! Do you know how proud I am of you?"

His reply? I AM PROUD OF ME TOO. (He even spelled it with a double "o"! This kid. Blowing our minds.)

What I noticed was that this was not just about school, for any of us. This was about facing what you have to face in order to go after what you want—*because* you want it. I could imagine how hard it was for Andrew to head to where he wanted to be, carrying with him the challenges he knew he'd have to face. It was beyond a heavy backpack. Andrew said as much. I believe he is far braver than most.

Feeling proud of you, Andrew, is an understatement. I am in awe.

"LOVE IS ALL."

−ANDREW

CHAPTER 20

Inclusion would become an ominous, elusive word for our family. Society prides itself on being inclusive but with no real idea how to do it (nor real investment to support it). *Or so has been our experience.* Hearts are in the right place, but that only goes so far. We need solutions. We need action. It is possible to have classrooms of students whose needs are supported alongside their peers. (All students have needs, and all students' needs should be supported, idealistic as that sounds.) Is it possible that not only do the children with support needs benefit but also that all students will? Of course it is.

For us, this is what inclusion looked like. But inclusion within a staff-stretched school and a resource-deficient school board looked different. One EA at a school with 575 kids meant our family, who could afford one parent with time-flexibility, could facilitate such inclusion. Clearly not *true* publicly funded inclusion, but we created an example nonetheless. Here I was, offering to show up to an offsite school event (a walkathon fundraiser for the school) in order to accompany my son and facilitate inclusivity. Me, moving beyond any expectation of what a school board *should* be doing in order to make "should" happen.

This is what happens with inclusion: Kids get a chance to see that, in fact, *we are all different.* Maybe we look different, or act differently, or communicate differently. Maybe it's obvious, maybe it's not. Maybe you have to see it, and be around it, and spend time in it. Maybe these kids end up learning that *different* is just a word. Maybe these inclusive kids grow up to be inclusive adults who accept that *different* is okay; in fact, it's necessary. *Different* is what creates a healthy, loving, compassionate society.

That day we participated in the school's morning walkathon fundraiser at a nearby park. Andrew walked the laps, on the periphery of his peers, a few friends popping over to say hi. Me, a few steps removed. Andrew took it all in. He was regulated enough to manage a full ten laps and the walk back to school. When we arrived at the classroom, I sat with Andrew for a debrief with his class. His teacher and I had discussed having me volunteer in the classroom in that capacity in order to facilitate a class discussion with Andrew. (I had run it by Andrew beforehand; he had spelled out yes to the opportunity to engage with his class.)

We asked if anyone had any questions for Andrew. One student's arm shot up. "What did you think of the walkathon, Andrew?" And with all eyes (about twenty-six sets) on him, Andrew spelled out, letter by letter:

IT WAS A LOT OF WALKING AND NOISE, BUT IT WAS GREAT BEING WITH ALL OF YOU.

You could hear a pin drop.

A room full of ten- and eleven-year-old minds busy processing, with surprised looks of "wow" and "okay, huh" on their faces. Not a snicker or a giggle. And then right back to the regular classroom buzz for lunch. The one student who had asked the question came over. She looked at me and said, "What Andrew wrote made me feel really happy." (The incredible reflective capacity and confidence of a ten-year-old!)

And I said, "Why don't you tell that to Andrew."

So, she turned to Andrew and said, "Um, Andrew, what you said on your board made me feel really happy."

And in Andrew fashion, he tilted his head to one side, eyes gazed afar, and smiled.

You can't script that kind of interaction. You can't write it into an education plan, or role play it as part of a class activity. That kind of exchange happens when kids have an authentic opportunity to experience inclusion firsthand. *That's* inclusion.

***

For weeks Andrew had been asking to join math class. It had been just over a month of him having attended school, and I could tell he wanted to spend more time there: he would bring me his backpack earlier in our morning routine. When I asked him what else he'd like to be part of at school, he would spell out "math" on his letterboard. Math. Grade six math. And not to say that Andrew didn't know math (he probably did), but we hadn't quite gone there yet. (There's a specific letterboard just for numbers and we had not yet had that training.) Dare I say that it was *only* one year prior that we had started contemplating school to begin with, let alone longer days. Let alone math class.

Math class? What would that look like? What would he *do* during math? (With no staff at his school having been trained on the letterboard, and his EA already limited in ways to engage him academically, I wondered what it would look like.) Clearly, Andrew was not worried.

"But Andrew, why math?" I asked him.

He carefully spelled out: MY BRAIN LOVES LOGICAL PROBABILITIES.

Stunned, I replied, "What does that even mean?"

And Andrew wrote: I LOVE NUMBERS AND FORMULAS.

So, we increased his day to include math class. And that's when he began walking around the house reading a math textbook. I kid you not. He'd hold it, then he'd sit down and flip through it. I would shake my head in awe, constantly, in those days.

This, as well as a documentary we had watched about a genius mathematician, got us thinking about how minds work differently. Andrew was with us when we viewed the film but was in and out of the room (his typical habit when watching something new on television). Of course, we knew he was taking it all in; in the past, we would have assumed that he was not paying attention.

The mathematician featured in the documentary read upward of fourteen books at a time with retention of content at about 90 percent. We thought it was quite phenomenal, so we asked Andrew, "The way this mathematician takes in information is unique. Do you relate to this?"

And, quite confidently, Andrew spelled out: YES. I SEE INFORMATION ON A PAGE AND I ENCODE IT INTO MY BRAIN.

Jaw-dropped, I laughed at the word *encode*. How did Andrew know what he knew?

This was our first window into how Andrew obtains information, and maybe, how he learns. Truthfully, it's Andrew who probably knows more about his mind than anyone else. And that's probably true of all nonspeaking autistic individuals, and yet we have tapped into none of it. We've made decisions about them without them. If we can appreciate that the autistic brain works differently, then surely we can entertain the idea that autistic individuals might acquire information differently. *How else does Andrew know what he knows?* We didn't read it to him, or spell it with him, or deliberately teach him. Much like the mathematician in the documentary who recognized that his thinking was unusual, Andrew commented, I KNOW I AM DIFFERENT.

Of course, I asked further: "How do you think you're different, Andrew?"

Letter by letter, he spelled out: I PROCESS THE WORLD DIFFERENTLY.

We balance a fine line with Andrew of wanting to learn everything we can about him and not wanting to push him too far.

I had to ask: "How do you know what you know?"

He looked at me like I should already know this about him. I HAVE BEEN READING WORDS SINCE I COULD HOLD A BOOK. It's true; he has held a book in his hands since he could walk.

"But how did you know what the words were? Or what they meant?"

YOU LEARN OVER TIME. PLUS, MY LISTENING ABILITY IS FAR SUPERIOR THAN AVERAGE.

I shook my head and continued. "But how do you know how to spell?" I'm bowled over.

I THINK ABOUT THE WORD IN MY MIND. I SEE THE LETTERS AND I PRACTICE PUTTING THEM IN ORDER IN MY MIND AND THEN I POINT THEM OUT ON MY BOARD AND I HOPE THEY COME OUT IN THE RIGHT ORDER.

I was honestly astounded. This felt like only the beginning of getting to know how Andrew's brain works, how he thinks, how he takes in the world. Clearly, there was so much to learn about the autistic experience, so much to learn about Andrew, from Andrew. And so much more ahead.

***

Over time, you learn to accept the life that is in front of you, *the life that is*. One of the hardest pieces for me to accept was that Andrew may never speak; that I might never hear his voice or hear the words *I love you*.

Sometimes, though, my brain imagines it differently. It is like a dream. In my mind, I hear him speak. My heart races, my throat is tight, my eyes well with tears, as if it is actually happening. In my mind, I am ecstatic. *Oh my goodness, my boy is talking! He is saying words!* I can hardly breathe. I am speechless.

His voice is sweet. So sweet. He says little things—I don't know what—a few soft little treasures. I see myself rush to him, falling to my knees, grabbing him, desperate to hear more. I'm crying absolute tears of joy like nothing I've ever cried before. It is the beginning of something new. And of finally learning things about my son I've never known before.

But then it's gone. It dissolves and I come out of it. Something brings me back—the dryer buzz, or Abby's little voice, or the smell of whatever I've been cooking as I daydreamed.

And it's okay. *It just is.*

Years ago we came to terms, to peace, with the fact that Andrew doesn't speak. We let go of any expectation, of any particular age, when we thought he might. We used to say, "Maybe he'll talk when he's four . . . Maybe by the time he's seven . . . " We decided to fully accept our child as he was *at present*–then, and now.

Do I imagine Andrew will speak one day? Honestly, I don't know. I can't say. I've let that go.

Would I love to hear his voice? And ask him questions and get answers? To be in conversation with him, like, *real* conversation (not just "Mama knows intuitively")? Sure, absolutely.

Do I think he is one of the most incredible people I know for traveling this many years in his body, navigating his world, taking all of life in without being able to speak? Most definitely.

And do I think his life has meaning? That his life matters? And that he *does* have something to say–he just says it without speaking? One hundred percent. For Andrew's autism gives him the inability to speak, but it also gives him one of the most beautiful voices I have ever heard.

When we let go, we allow for possibility. That's what I had done with his words–allowed for possibilities. And sometimes, the possibilities appear when we least expect them.

It was late October. Upon Abby's insistence, we got Andrew to sit on the couch with us so that we could ask him what he wanted to be for Halloween.

"Andrew, would you like to dress up for Halloween?" I asked him, to which he spelled out on his letterboard a very clear no. This was not surprising. Andrew had never liked Halloween. When he was eight, I stopped pushing. He was much happier being at home.

But Abby was still curious: "Is there *anything* you could dress up as, Andrew? Any ideas you have?"

Andrew wrote: N O T   R E A L L Y.

I added: "Abby thinks you need to go as something, Andrew, at least to school."

He replied, self-assuredly: I WOULD LIKE TO GO AS MYSELF.

He makes me laugh. He is so poignant, so clear and concise. Each time he expresses himself using the letterboard, I'm so happy for him, so proud. But that night, I got frustrated. "Andrew, sit up! Your arm keeps bumping your leg and you're not lifting your hand to hit the letters properly!" With this method, accuracy is everything. "Lazy spelling," as I call it, means the method won't work.

He looked hurt.

"Susan!" Stuart jumped in. "He's doing amazing! It's all amazing!"

He was right. It was all amazing. Sometimes I get caught up in where we're headed, or where I think we could be, versus how far we've come.

"I'm sorry, Andrew. I just always want this to work for you."

Andrew looked at me, lifted his hand and, unprompted, started pointing to the letters on the letterboard:

YOU HAVE BEEN SPELLING WITH ME ALL DAY. I LOVE YOU, MOM.

Holding the letterboard, I saw his words present in front of me, one by one, letter by letter. All I could do was smile. I didn't bawl my eyes out like I expected I would when I first "heard" those three words. I didn't scream. I just hugged him and smiled. It was casual, not contrived or prompted. Just your average conversation. Everything felt warm and beautiful.

I never thought I'd hear those words. Years ago I let all of that go. I vowed to live in the present rather than waiting for a future that wasn't mine. His words felt like recognition of that decision, proof of what happens when we truly let go, and of the gifts that present when we do.

"I WISH FOR THE DAY WHEN
EVERYONE MOVES FROM WORDS
TO HEARING WHAT IS
ALREADY AROUND THEM."

-ANDREW

CHAPTER 21

We managed to travel, over the years, our family. Sometimes all of us, sometimes just me and the kids. Sometimes, even, just me and Stu! In time, Stuart and I found that it was often easier, and almost more enjoyable, for us to have "solo trips": he with his cycling buddies—a trip to Europe, perhaps; me with any combination of girlfriends on a weekend getaway that included hiking, spa time, lots of laughs, and lots of tea (or prosecco, or both). But we made sure, as would the grandparents, that we always had time together as a couple.

The benefits outweighed the risks, but certainly, traveling with children was often stressful. Autism presents some real challenges. Eating out is hard. Crying babies nearby is excruciating for Andrew. And losing sight of your nonspeaking child, even for a split second, creates a surge of panic that makes your heart stop. Still, Stuart and I would decide it was worth it, if only for the change of scenery, warmth, and brighter days for Andrew (particularly through Toronto winters).

We often traveled to Mexico, to a less touristy town off the beaten path, where we'd been before.

On one particular trip, I was struck by Andrew's ability to experience pure joy. Abby experiences it naturally, automatically, playing in sand, shopping in markets, or just watching people walk by. But Andrew struggles so much with sensory overload that it often occludes him from experiencing what's around him. This trip was different. We watched Andrew deliriously laughing, swimming in the waves. We heard him humming loudly as we walked through the fruit stands. We saw him rocking and swaying, grinning as we drove our rented golf cart through the bumpy village streets. Yes, these were likely self-regulatory ways for Andrew to manage the intense sensory experience, but you could tell that he was also caught up in the pleasure of it all.

What struck me most was how present Andrew was. In fact, I'd never seen someone so fully *in the moment* as I did with Andrew. It doesn't matter who's watching, what else is going on, or what anyone thinks. Through observing Andrew, I have been shown the best example of what living in the present moment looks like. Allowing ourselves to experience joy—being in it *without condition*.

The curious thing about our time away with Andrew is how much he loves it—until he doesn't.

He loves to swim. He loves the sea. He loves to be outside. He gets to do all of that when we're away in Mexico. And it's familiar; we go to the same place where we've been a number of times before. Sometimes we even go with helpful grandparents. But by about day five or so, it flips. He cries more easily and shows outward signs of distress, like stomping his foot or banging his head against a tree. It's hard to watch. I feel for Andrew and I am conscious of strangers' looks.

In the past, we've played the guessing game. Is he too hot? Are things too loud? Were the waves too much? Is he bored? Hungry? Feeling left out?

"What is it, Andrew? What's wrong?" I might shout.

The fastest thing he can do is point to his chart of picture symbols. If he's beyond frustrated, though, he might just throw it. One particular instance, he pointed to "walk" which typically means he needs a break. So, we walked. We walked down the beach, then to a shady grove, and eventually, he walked us to the ferry terminal. At that point he was calm enough that I could ask him, *using his letterboard*, why we were there. He wrote:

I WISH WE WERE GOING HOME TODAY.

It doesn't get much clearer than that—except that, without the letterboard, I would have only been guessing.

"To the cold? Back to Canada?" I reply.

YES

"Not yet, Andrew. Soon—tomorrow." We walked back to where we were staying. He settled in, finding a quiet space and a book. I gave him some time before bringing out the letterboard again: "What happened out there, on the beach?" I asked him.

IT WAS ALL TOO MUCH.

"Can you give me an example of what was *too much?*"

Very deliberately, he wrote: THE WAVES, BABIES CRYING, BRIGHTNESS. . . . It's like he had a list. I HAVE HAD ENOUGH OF THE STIMULATION HERE.

Not surprising. There were colors and music and mopeds everywhere! "What do you need now, Andrew?"

And he spelled out: MY OWN SPACE. So, I left him.

Within an hour of getting what he needed, he came to me with his picture chart and pointed to "outside" and "swim." He was ready, restored.

None of this was new. We'd seen it before: the laughter, the stimulation, the meltdown. The difference was words—being able to express how he felt and what he needed, beyond the limits of a picture symbol. Having a voice and being heard. Perhaps being heard is most important of all. It is for most of us. Why wouldn't it be, then, for Andrew too?

***

Life felt like it was coming together. "This *is* happening," I would say, still marveling at the words coming out of my child. We were no longer guessing about Andrew's world. Yes, he still had his picture system of communication, which worked well for his basic needs and wants, but it was limited; *he* was limited. Now, Andrew had the chance to express more than what was printed on those picture symbols or programmed into his device.

We're finally accessing not only *what* he's wanting to say but the fact *that* he wants to say something in the first place. We don't take any of it for granted. Pointing to letters on a letterboard is harder than it looks. Eventually, it may lead to typing on a keyboard, but that is not necessarily the preference. Typing on a keyboard is not any less arduous; in fact, it can be even more taxing.

We live in a society that has put priority on spoken words—maybe words in general. Imagine not being able to communicate in the way society expects? And everyone around you misinterprets and underestimates you? The letterboard has given Andrew a voice in that world. He no longer feels like a silent observer in his own life. Now, he is a participant. I give so much credit to nonspeaking individuals like Andrew, having to navigate this life with such tolerance.

Andrew reminds us, though, that there is much that can be experienced beyond words. He writes about how he would like to just live in his senses without words interfering. When I ask where the words come from, he writes: E V E R Y O N E   E L S E . He was ten when he wrote: I   W I S H   F O R   T H E   D A Y   W H E N

EVERYONE MOVES FROM WORDS TO HEARING WHAT IS ALREADY AROUND THEM.

I marvel at this life now. I am in absolute awe watching it unfold.

We had our doubts that this communication method would work. As "autism parents," there is a vulnerability in having hope that something might make your child's life better—a therapy, a health program, or a means to communicate. You learn to protect your heart. The risk of disappointment, so great, if something isn't a fit, often quickly replaced by the tremendous guilt you feel for wishing that it would. There is a delicate balance between wanting more for your child and accepting them as they are.

Then, as if overnight, not only do you see your child exactly as they are, but the whole world sees them too.

As if life couldn't ascend any higher, three years into our letter-board journey, I received an email from one of Canada's largest autism advocacy organizations, asking us to present at their national conference. I read the email twice in disbelief. When Andrew came home from school that day, I asked him about the opportunity. He smiled and wrote yes on his letterboard. *How will a guy who doesn't speak present at an online conference?* Courageously, we accepted. We would figure this out too.

We poured hours into creating a twenty-five-minute video presentation. Comprised of video footage and pictures, as well as Andrew's words, Andrew's presentation gave a stunning and infor-mative window into his world. He titled it: "Life as a Nonspeaker: An Insider's Perspective." It aired on a Saturday morning, online, for Au-Some, Autism Canada's annual conference, among a dozen other live presentations. Thousands of people tuned in.

We received countless messages about the impact of Andrew's words. People learning for the first time that there was more to the face of nonspeaking autism. Families wanting to know how to get started with this method for their loved one. In fact, people were awestruck. (The presentation can still be viewed on YouTube.)

I AM UNABLE TO SPEAK. THESE ARE MY WORDS. I NEVER THOUGHT I WOULD EVER BE ABLE TO SHARE MY THOUGHTS WITH ANYONE. WAITING FOR SOMEONE TO FIGURE OUT THAT YOU ARE SMART IS VERY DIFFICULT. IT WAS YEARS BEFORE MY FAMILY DISCOVERED ME. PEOPLE KNOW I AM IN HERE. I FEEL REDEEMED. PEOPLE SEE ME AS MORE THAN JUST MY AUTISTIC BODY. I AM DESERVING OF THIS CREDIT AS ARE COUNTLESS OTHER AUTISTIC PEOPLE WHO HAVE NOT DISCOVERED OR PERSEVERED WITH THIS METHOD. IT TAKES BELIEF IN YOURSELF TOO.

We sat as a family on the couch, watching Andrew's words on our television screen. Stuart choked up, Abby beaming, and me, tears streaming down my face, shaking my head in awe. Andrew, too, who doesn't sit long for anything, sat and watched his whole part. He was proud—you could just see it. We were all proud.

As Andrew so eloquently shared in his presentation, autism presents some significant challenges. The letterboard doesn't take that away, but it allows for Andrew to better express himself and be understood through his own voice, not anyone else's.

I HAVE AN AUTISTIC BRAIN WHICH MAKES IT HARD FOR ME TO CONTROL MY BODY

EVEN THOUGH I AM SMART. I SOMETIMES DO REALLY STRANGE THINGS. I THINK WE ALL JUST WANT TO BE LOVED AS WE ARE, NO MATTER WHAT OUR CHALLENGES ARE.

Loved as we are. No truer words have ever been written.

PART III: ARISE

"HUMANS NEED TO PRACTICE
MORE COMPASSION
TOWARD EACH OTHER–
INCLUDING THOSE WHO
ANGER OR HURT THEM.
AND MOST ESPECIALLY,
THEMSELVES."

–ANDREW

CHAPTER 22

I have never wanted pity. I never wanted anyone to feel sorry for us. Yes, sympathy, compassion, and understanding, but not pity. I promised myself, through my raw and real sharing for our blog, *Life, Love & Autism*, that I would show the full picture, but never in an act of pity. And never at the expense of my child. I would uphold the decency of our family, always.

The truth is, it used to be very, very hard. Tears, rage, resentment. Cursing, yelling, arguments. Stress in our family, strain on our marriage. I would cry so hard and not know if I was sobbing in anger or despair. Some days I swore I'd never pick Andrew up from school. Some days I swore I'd never get through another day. And some days I just swore. Never did I doubt for a second that it was just as hard for Andrew—maybe harder. All those years.

Sometimes all you can do is put one foot in front of the other. Live out one day, then the next, and the next, until months and years have gone by and you realize just how far you've come. Then, only at that point, can you see the growth and recognize the pain.

It can still be hard for Andrew and for us. Andrew requires much support to perform day-to-day tasks, from getting dressed to putting a snack together to packing his school bag. Gains are made, but he will always require help. I'm realizing this is a lifelong dependency. I worry I should be doing more, teaching Andrew how to be more independent, how to *do more things*. I wonder about the future. I wonder what this will look like down the road.

Andrew doesn't stop moving. His body is in a constant state of motion in an effort to stay regulated; he has told us as much. Sometimes it's calm and rhythmic, but sometimes it's forceful and accelerated. It can feel like *we're* being pulled into his cyclone of movement and I want to yell "Stop moving! Just stop!" Andrew moves in this way to fulfill a need, the need for calm in his body or calm in his environment. Often, that is what he needs: to sit with someone (usually, it's Stuart; his company is calming), feel the pressure or presence of their body, and just be. Sometimes it's as though he's mirroring what we all need.

Like many families had told us, the teenage years have posed some real challenges. Andrew has experienced an increase in agitation and self-injury (head-banging on a wall or a tree; punching his chin) with puberty. He smashed his head so hard into a window one day at school that the tempered glass cracked into an intricate web of lines. Thankfully, he was okay, just a few cuts on his fingers from running his hand along the crackled glass. (It must have looked marvelous.) It had become apparent that Andrew was needing more support. Some days he would just sit and cry.

Back to my holistic roots, I researched natural support for puberty and teen mental health. Among other things, we began working with a functional medical doctor who prescribed medical cannabis for Andrew. Within six months of using CBD oil, Andrew was feeling more balanced, less volatile. As well, we reduced his time at school. Life became a juggle of time with me, Stu on weekends, as well as grandparents and hired partners who could go for hikes or drives with him, explore, move, and hang out. I felt hopeful about this new schedule. Andrew could decide how he wanted to spend his time. We could do online courses of interest and use the letterboard for meaningful participation.

Perhaps we could take road trips, visiting natural wonders and beautiful places.

There's no road map, though. There's no glimpse into what the journey will look like, or what lies ahead. As parents, we rely on instinct and intuition. Yes, now we have tools; the letterboard has given us a means to access what Andrew truly thinks and feels—but not always. Sometimes, like any teenager, he doesn't want to "talk." He pushes the letterboard away. The ability to know Andrew in ways beyond words, such as through body language and observation, often prevail. We have learned to love and accept *what is* and have found enjoyment within that. My hope is that this is reflected in the attitudes of others, but that is not always the case.

We were bullied at a park we'd been to many times before. We arrived, Andrew got out of the car, and in an unprovoked outburst of frustration, Andrew ran toward the trail, brushing an unsuspecting passerby. Alarmed, the man spun around at Andrew, shouting and swearing at him, an inch from his face. Intolerant, he yelled at me for raising "an a**hole of a child" and horridly suggested I put my "f*cking kid on a leash." Yes, a leash. Shocked, gutted, and tongue-tied, all I could say, with angry hot tears in my eyes, was "I hope you never have a child with a disability." I turned the corner and sobbed in anguish, heartbroken. I cried even harder when I grabbed Andrew and yelled, "Why can't you be normal? Just be normal!" The shame and disgrace of it all. I cried and cried and cried.

We had walked that path many times before and we will walk it again, but that day felt different. That day I walked with my head down, feeling the weight of all the years. I cried for the years that required tenacity and perseverance and strength. All the years of being brave. I cried for the times I had wished that

Andrew was different. Andrew, my ever-forgiving child walking behind me. Andrew, holding space for me and all my emotions, holding space for both of us. I cried because sometimes it's just so damn hard.

The man we encountered could have been anyone; he was all the ignorant, fragile, hurting people of the world. Not to excuse his behavior—maybe he was just a jerk—but I could tell that something wasn't quite right with him. He seemed "off."

When we got home, I asked Andrew about our encounter at the park. I wanted to know how he was feeling. Andrew, who hadn't been wanting to write much in those days, graciously spelled out:

SOME PEOPLE NEED LOVE EVEN MORE THAN YOU OR ME.

I cried again, because he was right. The only true antidote for hate and fear is love. Like needing to choose grace with ourselves, we need to choose to love others. Andrew, always seeing it through the lens of love, even where there is pain and challenge and hurt.

As Andrew writes: LOVE IS ALL.

I have learned through sharing in *Life, Love & Autism* how connected we are as human beings. Our stories matter. They are felt by one another, and they validate each of our experiences, the experience of being human.

In sharing our family's story, perhaps we are shifting the understanding of what it is to be human, to love, and to *be* love. In doing so, perhaps we are also shifting the perception of life with autism: that we each carry a purpose, and that the autistic mind brings a richness to life, something we can only perceive when we consider that life itself can be experienced in a different way.

***

For a long time, I cringed at the word *disability*. The "D" word. Eventually, it became easier for me to say "I have a child with a disability" than to say "disabled child." I would even substitute with other terms like "differently abled" or "varied abilities."

I'm not sure why it was hard for me. It still is. And it's all my own stuff; I'm making the word mean something sad or tragic or *less than*—or society has and I've taken that on. I worked so hard for so many years at seeing my child as more than what society sees (or how they treat people with disabilities). I worked hard at acceptance. More recently, I worked hard to raise him up and give him the credit he deserves, having been so grossly underestimated.

All of that still stands, but when it is stripped away, there is still disability. By definition, "dis-ability" is an ability to do or be in another way. We see that. We have always seen that. This is neither good nor bad; disability is neutral. *It just is.* Somedays it depends on the color lens we look through. We experience the joy of being Andrew's parents *and* are still dealing with the challenges of navigating that very path. It is both.

Andrew is busy. He doesn't stop moving. He needs extensive bike rides and hikes and swims to help his body self-regulate (including for sleep). Too much time inside or in confined spaces makes him spin. He doesn't sit with an iPad anymore (and that's fine!) or watch shows or play video games. He used to flip through books and magazines, sometimes for hours. He doesn't now.

He breaks things. He picks all the leaves off my garden plants. He throws objects over our fence. Sometimes he has to put everything in sight away. He knows it's "weird" (his word), and he doesn't know why he does it. And it will change—it always does. Sometimes it's for attention. Sometimes he's bored. And sometimes he's just being a pain—like many teenagers! We comprehend that, except that *this is part of* disability.

My holistic brain is wired to see *the whole*, or the gift, in disability. Am I doing a disservice to myself, and more so, to Andrew, for thinking this way? Possibly. Part of me believes that his disability allows him tremendous ability in other ways, such as to see things simply for what they are.

He is independent and hugely dependent. He is adventurous and nonsensical. He is handsome and funny and bright. He is incredible. He navigates his life without speaking—with a brain-body disconnect. He is brilliant and he is disabled. Can it be all of these things? And can that be okay?

Perhaps this is what makes the highs so triumphant. Like the day Andrew learned to ride his bike, or the day we heard his voice through the letterboard, or the day he told his sister "I love you." I find myself in tears at it all. I see Andrew, a highly sensitive, intuitive, *disabled* able person, as a being of light. A beautiful child of creation. Perfectly intended.

So here I am, me, his mother, struggling in her humanness, seeking to love and accept and uphold her child, and in those very torn moments, what comes to me is this:

You can know this is your soul's journey (and your child's) *and* acknowledge that it is really hard. You can believe you were gifted this path *and* feel burdened by it. You can work to accept this life *and* resist or resent it. It is all good, and hard, and we are all just walking our paths the best we know how.

In time, I will accept the word disability as just another word in the language that we use to describe life: our bodies, our minds, and what it is to be human. I will accept that disability is not a swear word.

"FORGIVENESS IS WHEN I LET GO
OF WHAT I THINK YOU SHOULD
HAVE DONE AND RECOGNIZE THAT
YOU ARE ONLY HUMAN, AS AM I."

-ANDREW

CHAPTER 23

School continues to be one of the most challenging pieces to navigate in Andrew's life. Andrew wants to be there but finds it hard to manage. We want him to be there but find that the level of support to meet his needs falls short. Andrew (and others like Andrew) are cognitively capable *and* need help with self-regulation and access to meaningful communication in order to benefit from what school offers. Nonspeaking autistic students like Andrew have a desire to learn and have a right to access education but are completely underestimated and poorly accommodated in public education. We see Andrew with huge potential and opportunities for growth and yet unable to reach them, partly due to limitations within the school system, a system so standardized that it does not allow for differences. But partly, it's Andrew.

Always in the back of my mind is the quest to find the most ideal place for Andrew to spend his time. I imagine it as an outdoor school, one where he can be in the trees and self-regulate through nature. I love the idea of him being with kids in our community—whether that's truly best for him or what feels best for me. I love the ideal of an inclusive society, of an inclusive classroom. I also know he requires intensive support. Does this exist? Can all of it come together? Can I create this for him? Like most parents of children with exceptionalities, I am always searching.

I have spent hours researching public and private school options for Andrew. Sometimes it seems like there is nowhere for Andrew to go. Where does a bright kid who can't speak, who requires access to his most meaningful method of communication—the letterboard—and who needs support, belong? Hard to imagine that in a city as big as Toronto, Canada, there aren't a lot of options.

He could continue at the autism center, learning life skills and expanding his use of LAMP (the picture-to-voice output system on his iPad, which he can use with anyone). As well, the center has been an important source of respite for us, but, as Andrew has attended since he was four, he's *over it.* He knows how smart he is. He is being taught ABCs and 123s with a mind capable of poetry and algebra using those very same letters and numbers. Trapped in his body like so many of the bright autistic kids who attend autism centers, his growth there is limited. They don't support the use of the letterboard at the center and I suspect they never will.

He could continue at our local school: age-level curriculum and learning, with kids his age, feeling part of the community. We could continue to work tirelessly to advocate to have the letterboard method in school, given it is Andrew's most meaningful way to express his knowledge and opinions and allow for him to participate in class discussions. We can hope that the bureaucracy we have encountered within the school board does not prevent Andrew from exercising his right to access education and communication.

He could go to private school. Not all private schools are open to having someone attend who requires significant support (and because it's private, they can choose to make such brazen exclusions), but if they valued diversity, we could pay their tuition, pay to have a 1:1 worker with Andrew, and pay to train their staff to use the letterboard. Unfeasible as that sounds, I felt hopeful with one prospective school. But as the conversation with the director continued, I knew it would no longer be a fit.

"We don't think that your child can learn here, at our school, without any language," the director said to me in trying to understand what the letterboard method of communication was all about.

"Of course he is capable of learning!" I retorted, but the conversation was already over. The director muttered words like "your child would add a layer to our school" and "we can't" and "we just don't," and I wished I had recorded the conversation for proof of how audacious the words of *those who think they know what's best* can be. This, from the head of admissions at a private school that prides itself on diversity and inclusion, in Canada's largest city. A school where no amount of money can buy your child the opportunity to learn.

One of many similar conversations, this one left me completely discouraged and disillusioned—and enraged. I hung up and swore I would never spend a penny on a school that didn't presume competence in my child.

My child *can* learn and *does* learn and *is* cognitively capable. Andrew says it best himself:

BEING A NONSPEAKER MEANS YOU ARE CONSTANTLY TONGUE-TIED. YOU HAVE TO STAND WITNESS TO EVERYTHING GOING ON AROUND YOU AND OFTEN JUST LET IT BE. EXCRUCIATING AT TIMES. WE EXPERIENCE LANGUAGE AND COMPREHENSION IN OUR BRAIN THAT DOES NOT GET EXPRESSED THROUGH SPEECH, BUT WE DO HAVE VERBS!

HENCE, WE PREFER THE TERM NONSPEAKING (OVER NONVERBAL). PEOPLE NEED TO KNOW THAT WE ARE SMART, THAT WE EXPERIENCE EMOTIONS, AND THAT WE WISH TO HAVE PURPOSE AND PARTICIPATE IN SOCIETY JUST LIKE EVERYONE ELSE.

And so I became an unwavering advocate for my child. I vowed I would never, ever quit fighting for my child's right to access support, accommodation, inclusion, education, and communication. The trailblazing path of advocacy that lay ahead for our family would be paved by Andrew's influence and the experience of other nonspeakers. "Nothing about us, without us."

***

Imagine having to prove yourself? Prove that you are cognitively capable? Prove that you are capable of producing words (thoughts, opinions)—words that are your own, not anyone else's? The publicly funded education system in Ontario leaves families no choice; this is the level to which we are reduced in order to have Andrew optimally accommodated and included at school.

Perhaps like it is for many parents who first learn of the letterboard, it seems unimaginable and counterintuitive to autism personnel within the school board, superintendents and chiefs alike, that the nonspeaking autistic person might have something to say. Vastly underestimated, Andrew and his fellow nonspeakers are forced to prove that they warrant (and deserve) accommodations beyond what the school boards have traditionally provided. The letterboard tool for communication, with its requirement for an accompanying communication and regulation partner, is not commonly known nor readily adopted by the systems that claim to support the nonspeaking autistic population.

Seeing Andrew spell on the letterboard is something you can't unsee.

I remember the first time I watched a "speller" spell out his name, letter by letter, on a letterboard—just his name alone had me astounded, embarrassingly; I had no idea our nonspeaking children were so cognitively capable. I was in disbelief, but not in a way that I doubted what I had seen—disbelief that everything I thought I knew about my own nonspeaking child would have to be unlearned and relearned. Now this is what we expect of everyone—doctors, teachers, specialists, everyone: to undo and redefine their understanding of nonspeaking autism. Ah, the privileged position of a self-appointed group of "experts" determining another group's authenticity, identity, and worth.

Yet here we are, being told we need studies and data to validate what families like ours see with their own eyes, what we *know* is working for our child. Our family gathered that proof: the gold standard Psycho-Educational Assessment. Hours and hours of testing, an arduous assessment of learning style, cognitive processing and ability, academics, and so on. We weren't required to pursue this testing, we chose to. We found a supportive clinician in Toronto and allocated the time and resources ourselves.

This clinical psychologist presumes competence. Her method of practice validates the utilization of the letterboard in order to gather true representative data in nonspeaking autistic individuals. Ordinarily, most nonspeakers do not excel in these assessments as most of the testing requires a neuro-physical motor ability to complete tasks that involve writing, building, and pointing, with which many autistic individuals struggle. Thus, unrepresentative conclusions are often made about the cognitive ability of nonspeakers by clinicians who do not allow use of the letterboard in this type of assessment.

It is worth noting that research is actively underway, validating what families know to be true of their nonspeaking loved ones. Research on eye-tracking and eye-gaze is emerging with promising results, formulating proof that nonspeaking individuals can and do acquire foundational literacy skills. Continued research will affirm the experiences of nonspeaking individuals who use the letterboard for greater access, autonomy, and agency in their lives. Hopefully, this research will change the trajectory of even more lives across the globe.

At the start of the assessment, we asked Andrew what he was hoping to get out of the experience. He replied, letter by letter, without hesitation:

I HAVE ALWAYS STATED THAT NONSPEAKING AUTISTICS DESERVE THE CREDIT THEY HAVE BEEN WITHOUT FOR THEIR ENTIRE LIVES. MAYBE THE OBSERVATION BY SKILLED AND RESPECTED PROFESSIONALS WILL GIVE CREDIT WHERE CREDIT IS DUE.

There is a whole community of nonspeakers defending their ability to learn, to think for themselves, and to be able to share all of who they are. They shouldn't have to, but most nonspeakers want nothing more than to have their voices heard, their voices validated.

The clinical psychologist was in awe, humbled by what Andrew was capable of through this method. Yet every week Andrew sits in a classroom without access to his letterboard or a trained communication and regulation partner because the school board is looking for "proof." This desire to validate any new method comes from wanting to assess the "risk versus benefit"—not just for one child, but for every child for whom this method might apply. What is made available to one child must also be made possible for another. This is time-consuming, involves many people rethinking educational models and paradigms, and is, above all else, costly for school boards.

Tempted as I am to send in the letterboard every day as an expectation of its use, I hold the power of this communication tool in such high regard that I would never want it misused, falling short of its purpose and potential, and then misinterpreted as a tool that "doesn't work." It requires hours of training and best practice, not to mention the development of a trust bond between Andrew and his communication and regulation partner. As Andrew says, I NEED TO TRUST THE PERSON WITH MY WORDS. MY WORDS ARE EVERYTHING.

Andrew demonstrated that he is cognitively above average for his age and grade level. Ninety-ninth percentile for vocabulary. Above average in the areas of language, cognitive reasoning, and math. Not surprisingly, he struggles with spatial tasks involving brain-to-hand coordination, overall independence, and life skills. In sum: a very bright teenager with significant support needs. *How does a school board accommodate this?* There is a growing number of families who are coming to the same conclusion.

I think back to the very first time Andrew was assessed for his cognitive ability, back when this journey began. I cringe. It was the very first time someone told me my child was "less than"–that one test, back when Andrew was only three and I was blindsided by the process. I watched as the early interventionists assessed my child based on questions he couldn't answer, with words he didn't have, or a pencil he couldn't hold. I stood there, holding back tears of anger, disdain, and sorrow. I watched them score blank answer after blank answer, equating Andrew's *cognitive ability* to his ability to be tested. He scored in the lowest percentile. I never did finish reading their report.

Almost ten years later, I am stunned by my child's ability, now validated by the results of an educational assessment. *And should I be?* Should we not be primed with the notion, when our children are first diagnosed with "severe nonverbal autism," that they may actually be cognitively *able*? Encouraged by "the experts" to presume competence in our children? Should I be this surprised, this amazed, that my child is as bright as he is? How do we not know this?

This, however, quickly becomes a prickly topic. Does valuing and esteeming cognitive ability in an otherwise underestimated population cause injustice and divide within the disability community as a whole? Does it mean we are devaluing those with cognitive challenges or disability? Not supporting or accepting someone, regardless of ability? What does this say of me as a parent? Does it mean I needed there to be "more" to my child? Does this evaluated depth of my child's ability mean I put greater worth on him? For me, it is none of that. It is purely the delight in learning more about my child. And, perhaps, the validation of what I knew to be true: that Andrew was, in fact, present in his mind in a way that no one could access or connect with.

We are merely, through use of the letterboard tool for communication, providing the nonspeaking community with the opportunity for access, autonomy, and agency that they have long deserved.

Still, Andrew receives no access to his most meaningful, purposeful tool for communication at school. This, the same child who self-advocated to attend "regular school." The same child who received the Courage Award two years in a row from his elementary school principal. Years of advocating for Andrew's right to access meaningful communication and we find ourselves up against a brick wall, still not supported by Canada's largest school board. The letterboard does not appear in a drop-down menu of AAC tools from which autism support staff can choose; schools don't know what to do with it; teachers want to use it but aren't supported.

In grade seven, Andrew's teacher (who was open-minded and honoring of Andrew but restricted by school board bureaucracy) asked the class for their response to the Robert Frost poem "The Road Not Taken." Andrew wrote his reflection at home, using his letterboard, then brought his words to school for a classmate to read aloud. It read:

THE PATHS IN THIS POEM ARE REPRESENTATIVE OF LIFE. I WOULD THINK THAT MOST OF US WILL ENCOUNTER TIMES IN OUR LIFE WHEN WE HAVE A CHOICE. WE CAN CHOOSE WHAT IS FAMILIAR, BUT WE CAN ALSO CHOOSE TO BE BRAVE AND TRY SOMETHING NEW. WHEN WE TAKE THE WAY THAT IS LESS FAMILIAR, WE MAY DISCOVER SOMETHING TRULY AWESOME FOR OURSELVES. BEING AUTISTIC IS LIKE TAKING THE ROAD LESS TRAVELED. IT IS A LESS KNOWN WAY OF LIVING WITH LOTS OF DISCOVERIES ALONG THE WAY.

Andrew's brilliance outshines any dead-end path. His perseverance surmounts the roadblocks. His patience allows us to pursue the road less traveled.

At some point I accepted that it was in our best interest to surrender: not to give up, but to let go of what clearly wasn't changing, and to make decisions that were of most benefit to us. It was never the principal, or the teacher, or any of the support staff holding us back. It was bureaucracy itself—giant educational systems tied up in red tape, holding themselves and the students they serve back from looking at new methods and seeing outside the box. Systems that serve the masses, not ones that are programmed to meet the needs of the individual child.

This was never about blame; this *is* about moving forward.

In an ideal world, our children would be part of a system that meets their needs, the needs of each individual; a system that was open to new ideas, new methods (like the letterboard tool for communication); a system that was willing to do things differently. It would include families that value learning beyond just *knowledge*—relevant learning, applied learning, experiential learning. A system open to external consultation and participation. Resourceful, not inefficiently stretched or strapped by resources. One based on a society that upholds and invests in children. Ideally, a system that supports the whole of a child: physical, mental, emotional, and spiritual. One that includes fresh air, time in nature, discovery, activity, movement, nutrition, breathing, mindfulness, stillness, and space. Nourishment on all levels. Totally idealistic—a vision of the world I wish to see.

What does *Andrew* want? He writes:

I WANT TO LEARN ABOUT THE THINGS THAT MATTER, LIKE LOVE AND OPENNESS AND ONENESS. WE LEARN THAT BEYOND THE WALLS OF SCHOOL. WE LEARN THAT THROUGH LIVING.

The path is ours.

"KEEP SHOWING UP."

-SUSAN

CHAPTER 24

It hasn't always been easy being Andrew's dad. Stuart is the first to admit this. Taking your autistic child out in the community comes with its risks and challenges. Stuart missed out on Little League and extracurriculars at school. In the beginning, when you think of all you're *supposed* to be doing with your child, it stings. (Now Stuart doesn't mind as much. A lot of the extracurriculars just make life busy.)

Always a provider, Stuart built a foundation for growth, including for Andrew. Stuart's relationship with Andrew deepened as Andrew got older, but it was not until Andrew was able to connect on a level with words that Stuart truly had his heart opened. Seeing Andrew on the letterboard shook Stuart's whole understanding of who he had known his son to be. He felt guilty, apologetic, and then reignited in his role as Andrew's father. Through a newfound admiration of his son and all Andrew had endured in the years when no one, including his family, had truly known who he was, Stu was committed. Yes, there would still be challenges in raising an autistic son, but for Stuart, it was all in knowing that there was love there. Love and understanding.

What has transpired over the years is nothing short of spectacular: a true bond between father and son. Not the type that shares long chats or trades sports facts, but deep, meaningful love. An unspoken love, adoring and mutual. A love full of understanding, respect, and lots of laughter. Stu is good for that—always making Andrew laugh.

Andrew wrote his dad a message for Father's Day one year, thirteen years in the making. His words made every hard moment worth it.

I LOVE YOU, DAD. YOU ARE A GREAT PERSON IN MY LIFE. I AM SO GLAD I PICKED YOU TO BE MY DAD. IT IS A HARD JOB, MAYBE HARDER THAN YOUR ACTUAL WORK! YOU HAVE GROWN IN PATIENCE OVER THE YEARS. THANK YOU.

LOVE, ANDREW

Being able to share his cycling passion with Andrew was a dream come true for Stuart. A slightly different version than perhaps what he envisioned when he first propped Andrew up as a toddler on a tricycle, the two of them now go for trail rides, street rides, and "real rides." (Stuart grins when he uses the term "real rides"–pure glee–as that's the hard kind of mountain biking they do together.)

Andrew once wrote:

MY BIKE REPRESENTS ME. I SEE IT HAVING HUGE POTENTIAL FOR ADVENTURE AND FREEDOM, KIND OF LIKE ME. I AM OTHERWISE STUCK IN MY AUTISTIC BODY, BUT WHEN I USE MY WORDS, I AM LIKE MY BIKE: FREEDOM TO BE MYSELF AND SEE WHERE THE WORLD TAKES ME. I CAN INTERACT WITH THE WORLD ON MY BIKE. RIDING MY BIKE IS A HUGE ACCOMPLISHMENT, LIKE MOST THINGS I HAVE TO WORK HARD AT.

He had written this piece for his grade seven class. Each student had been asked to share something that best represents them. Bike riding is one of Andrew's favorite activities: he can be outside, in nature, moving his body. Maybe Stuart sees himself in Andrew's words too.

It had been more than five years of spelling to communicate using the letterboard, and not a day had gone by when we weren't grateful for it and all of Andrew's words. Not a single day. It had become a very powerful tool in our life.

I would ask myself: *Are words really necessary?* We had grown in our acceptance of what was. We had come to love this life and cherish our family as we were. We had an unspoken connection, an intuitive knowing. At some point, though, I acknowledged that Andrew's words mattered to me as much as I expected they mattered to him. Words gave Andrew the agency and autonomy that his disability otherwise denied him. Words felt like everything.

Through the letterboard, we learned that the act of being in his body, coordinating his own movements, and the ability to navigate his physical environment, were tasks unto themselves. So, for years, we have persevered with teaching him physical skills like using a seatbelt, putting on Velcro shoes, and learning to ride a bike.

Enter: skiing.

Can you imagine the motor coordination required to master the physical act of skiing? We started with adapted ski lessons when Andrew was young, using a harness and balance poles. Stuart, always alongside Andrew, coaching the instructors on how best to engage with Andrew until, eventually, Stuart took over. Now, it was just Andrew and his dad.

Let me say that teaching your *disabled child* requires a lot of pride and a whole lot of patience. When the stakes are high, and your desire for your child to *get it* is even higher, there is plenty of room for disappointment and frustration, maybe even injury.

It has taken years.

It began with skiing in tandem. Andrew would hold on to Stuart's poles, outstretched across his waist. Andrew couldn't stop on his own, so, skiing two abreast, Stuart would carefully navigate the descent amid all the other (typically novice) skiers on the hill. They practiced on beginner (green) runs in Ontario, then one year, set forth to ski a mountain: Mont Tremblant in Quebec. They have never looked back. It has been one of the most momentous achievements to date, particularly for Stu who loves to ski and carried the task of teaching Andrew.

One day, when I saw Andrew lingering by his letterboard after a full morning of skiing, I knew he must have something to say. Like with all motor tasks, initiating use of the letterboard *himself* did not come easily, so I had to seize the moment.

"Andrew, do you need to say something on your letterboard?" And when he didn't vocalize "no" ("nah," as he says), I took it as a yes.

I held up his letterboard.

I DON'T THINK YOU HAVE ANY IDEA WHAT A MASSIVE FEAT IT IS FOR ME TO SKI. THE AMOUNT OF MOTOR PLANNING REQUIRED TO GET MY BODY TO GO WHERE I WANT IT TO AND DO WHAT I WANT IT TO IS OVERWHELMING. MY BRAIN HEARS MY DAD GIVING ME INSTRUCTIONS AND I WILL MY BODY SO HARD TO PRACTICE THAT MOTION OR MOVEMENT. SOMETIMES AFTER OVER AND OVER PRACTICE I GET THE MOTOR PATH. SOMETIMES I NEVER GET IT, STILL, AND I WANT TO SCREAM BUT MY BODY WON'T LET ME DO THAT EITHER.

We were all silent. Me, overcome by his words, his aware-ness, his tenacity, and his humanness. His dad, hearing what he imagined was the truth for his son. His sister, so unconditionally proud of her older brother. We held him, hugging him with praise, acknowledging the huge mountain he had literally just surmounted.

He loves it and is so proud of himself.

This is why we persist as Andrew's parents. *This* is why we don't accept "nah" or protests or even head-banging (at first). Because, at first, it is *all* hard, for Andrew and for us. It is hard to learn the motor planning to execute a complex body task like skiing (or biking, or jumping, for that matter). And it is easy, really easy, to quit. Andrew knows this. We know this. But we keep showing up.

Time and time again I am reminded of how powerful it is to "just" show up. Because just showing up means you face the obstacle. Just showing up allows you to see the path and take the next step. Just showing up shows you that that's all it takes: try, fall, get up, practice, repeat. Oh, and cry, throw your poles, and call it a day sometimes. All of us.

Keep showing up.

And so, we do. We keep showing up. Stu, me, our family. One day at a time, one foot in front of the other. So much of the success in this life is due to our ability to show up. Where does that come from, the drive, the spark, the energy to show up? I believe it's within us—something we learn is there through having dusted off our knees after falling many times before. Life teaches us that we can do this, but we have to live it to learn it, to be shown our capacity to keep showing up.

"WHEN I AM PRESENT
IN MY BODY, I AM PRESENT
TO EVERYTHING ELSE."
−ANDREW

CHAPTER 25

Sometimes, even when life feels manageable, the unexpected occurs. Like when I lost Andrew.

I lost my nonspeaking autistic teenager who confidently (and maybe defiantly) does *not* always respond to his name, like in the case when I, his mother, beckoned repeatedly for him while he was happily strolling, on his own, through the brush of a Toronto park that he'd been to countless times before.

For nearly an hour (or what felt like an eternity), Andrew was missing. He was thirteen. At first, I didn't really think it was happening. I went into adrenaline mode, retracing the twenty steps I might have gained from where we were last together, where Abby and I last saw him playing in the leaves. But we weren't finding him. I called Stuart to meet us at the park. I gave Stuart fifteen minutes to comb the park on his bike before I called the police. Stuart found Andrew along a side trail at the exact moment the police arrived; Andrew was fine, listening to the flick of an oak leaf by his ear.

"No, he doesn't run away. Yes, I remember what he was wearing. No, he's not likely to be in distress when you find him," I had said to the police when I called. This was on the heels of a particularly volatile week—probably the toughest it had been for us since Andrew was diagnosed with autism almost ten years prior. He had been getting into things and was being silly and mischievous.

I told myself to breathe. I played it all out in hindsight: He must have taken a different footpath from where we were, and when

Abby and I circled back to find him, he had continued to move forward, gaining ground. It was awful, though I knew we would find him. My gut said he was still in the park . . . somewhere. But in the final minutes before he was found, I admit, my mind wandered. I started to feel sick. My legs went numb. I shook my head, choked up, and cried softly, "I can't do this anymore. I just can't." And that's when the call came through that he had been found.

It was a nonchalant reunion, surprisingly. Andrew seemed unfazed, which softened both my and Stuart's immediate parental reaction of "You can't leave us like that!" and "We're so glad you're okay!" Hugs, then back to the car.

I had held it together for Abby. (I crumbled in the hours and days that followed; we had been in "fight or flight" mode for a while by that week.) Tripping on roots as we hustled along the paths looking for her brother, Abby cried quiet tears. "But Mama, *will* we find him? What if we don't find him? What if he can't find *us*?" Abby's little heart was beating so fast when I finally stopped to hug her. My beautiful girl. I told her we would find him. We would, somehow. And if we didn't, well, we would deal with that too. We stopped people along our search, enlisting them in finding Andrew. We called the police. We prayed. It all brought me to a place of seeing "the big picture" pretty quickly.

It's amazing what the human body is capable of in those moments. What the mind is capable of. And what the human spirit feeds on in order to survive. Absolutely, in many ways, we were lucky. I say that Andrew had all his guardian angels–his people–looking out for him. He, of course, lives in a world of faith and trust that all is well, that all will be okay, always. And often, it is.

If you ask Andrew, which we did, he was never missing—he was at home in the trees. Yes, he knew it was scary for us, but he wasn't worried. Hmm, easy for you to say, Andrew! (Yes, we ended up getting an ID tag sorted for Andrew, and no, he was not wearing his MedicAlert bracelet that at least would have identified him as nonspeaking and linked him to an emergency database!) Again, we felt lucky and protected.

Weeks later, I was still processing the emotions of losing him, finding him, and admitting that I couldn't do "this" anymore. *What does that even mean?* Because of course I would do it, still. It meant I was looking at life and solutions and support from a wider perspective. Where could I enlist extra help? Who could I hire to be a "big brother" to Andrew? Would a service animal be beneficial—to Andrew, or even, to me?

Interestingly, Andrew had written an insightful piece about what life was like being him. His words were a window into the duality of his autistic experience. Letter by letter, it all made sense.

MAKE NO MISTAKE, MY LIFE IS FULL OF CHALLENGE LIVING IN THIS WORLD. IT IS FULL OF SENSORY OBSTACLES TO OVERCOME AND IS FULL OF BUSY PEOPLE DISCONNECTED FROM THEIR SOURCE. I WAS BORN KNOWING I AM A CHILD OF CREATION AND HAVE REMAINED CONNECTED TO WHAT MATTERS. LOVE, COMPASSION, FORGIVENESS ARE WHAT MATTER MOST. LIVING IN A WORLD WHERE PEOPLE ARE ONLY JUST COMING TO REMEMBER THAT THIS IS WHAT LIFE IS ALL ABOUT IS HARD. IT IS LIKE I AM THE ONLY ONE SEEING LIFE IN ITS TRUE COLORS—AN

AMAZINGLY RICH WORLD BUT LONELY SOMETIMES.

BEING IN MY ACTUAL BODY, I FEEL EVERY SINGLE THING. I FEEL MY BLOOD PUMPING IN MY VEINS AND ARTERIES. I FEEL MY BRAIN CELLS FIRING. I FEEL MY THROAT VIBRATE WHEN I MAKE MY SOUNDS. I FEEL MY MUSCLES FLEX WHEN I MOVE AND I LOVE IT! I FEEL MY HAIR BLOW IN THE WIND. MOST IMPORTANT, I FEEL MY FEET ON THE GROUND WHEN I STAND STILL. (IT IS HARD FOR ME TO STAND STILL.)

I ALSO RECOGNIZE THAT YOU MAY NOT UNDERSTAND WHAT IT IS LIKE TO BE ME. MY WORLD SEEMS STRANGE TO YOU. YOU DON'T SEE WHAT I SEE. I HEAR WHAT YOU DON'T HEAR. WE FIND ENJOYMENT IN DIFFERENT THINGS. I THINK THAT'S FINE BECAUSE WE ARE DIFFERENT PEOPLE. I FIND AMUSEMENT IN SIMPLE THINGS. YOUR WORLD SEEMS MORE COMPLICATED. I HAVE LIMITED INTERESTS IN YOUR EYES BUT IN MINE I AM CONTENT. MY BOREDOM COMES FROM NOT BEING INCLUDED OR NOT BEING CHALLENGED.

AND OF COURSE WE LIVE IN THE SAME WORLD, BUT OUR EXPERIENCE OF THE WORLD IS DIFFERENT. YOU SEEM TO EXPERIENCE THE MORE DENSE ASPECTS, LIKE COMPETITION AND ENVY AND HATRED, WHICH CAUSE DIVIDE

AND A DISCONNECT TO YOUR TRUE SELF. I EXPERIENCE THE LIGHTER ASPECTS, LIKE LOVE AND EMPATHY AND BEAUTY, WHICH KEEP ME CONNECTED TO MY HIGHER SELF.

FOR MANY YEARS, PEOPLE DIDN'T KNOW I WAS IN HERE. THOSE WERE SOME OF THE HARDEST YEARS. CAN YOU IMAGINE?

THE HARDSHIP OF LIVING IN THIS BODY IS ALSO THE GIFT. IT IS AWFUL AT TIMES BUT IS ALSO THE WAY FOR MY SOUL TO GAIN WHAT IT IS HERE TO LEARN: COMPASSION FOR THOSE WHO EXPERIENCE THE WORLD IN WAYS DIFFERENT FROM ME. AND OF COURSE UNCONDITIONAL LOVE FOR MYSELF AND FOR OTHERS.

WOULD I TRADE IT AT TIMES? YES. BUT IT IS MY LIFE TO LIVE, MOST DEFINITELY.

***

For as long as I can remember, Andrew has been interested in my eyes. Actually, he's been interested in a lot of people's eyes–his teachers', his grandparents', even strangers'–but mostly mine.

He would point repeatedly to his own eyes until I would say something like "Eyes!" And if that wasn't it (because he wouldn't let up), then I would try other phrases like "Andrew's eyes," "Your eyes," "I see you." Nope, not those either. "Mama's eyes" was often satisfactory. Of course, in due time, I was able to ask him with the letterboard.

"Andrew, you keep pointing to your eyes and mine. What would you like me to say? What would you like to talk about?"

His answer: THE SOUL. My wise old soul.

"Okay, so why don't you continue. Tell me about the soul." And while it took a few sittings, he quite literally spelled it all out for me—for *all of us* actually. He wants his words shared. He made that very clear to me early on when I told him that I shared stories about our family through our blog, *Life, Love & Autism*.

THE EYES HOLD EVERYTHING TO SEE INTO ANOTHER'S SOUL. BUT REMEMBER TO FEEL IT TOO. FEEL WHO THEY ARE. EVEN WHEN WE ARE WITH OTHERS AND NOT ABLE TO SEE THEIR FACES, AND SO, CANNOT READ THEIR EXPRESSIONS, WE CAN FEEL WHAT IT MEANS TO BE WITH THEM. DOES IT FEEL GOOD OR COMFORTABLE OR UNEASY OR SAD OR INCREDIBLE.

He writes this as he is squeezing my hand with his, rocking, and making happy sounds. He can hardly contain himself. He continues.

WHAT I HAVE LEARNED IS THAT IT HAS ALWAYS BEEN IMPORTANT TO DO THIS. TO FEEL PEOPLE. IT IS NOT ABOUT SPEECH OR WORDS THAT COME OUT. IT IS A FEELING FROM ONE SOUL TO ANOTHER. THIS IS WHY WE ARE HERE. TO RECONNECT. ALLOWING OURSELVES TO BE FREE TO BE OURSELVES. AND ALLOWING OTHERS.

Andrew has always had an ability to connect with others. It may have been hard to describe, hard to identify, but it was there. He could tease his grandparents, even as a toddler, rattling Poppa's wine bottle collection once he knew he had his attention or by hiding Grandma's hat. It was all very deliberate; Andrew was connecting.

One Christmas, about two years into the letterboard method, Andrew wrote some of the people in his life a note. We worked on these notes for weeks. Abby watched as Andrew wrote messages to his teachers, a few friends, his dad. Then one day Abby quietly whispered to me, "Maybe he can write *me* a note." My lovely Abby.

For years Abby has had to navigate an atypical sibling relationship. "Does he even like me, Mama?" she would ask. He would hardly pay any attention to her. Many times, when they were little and things were very hard, he would either cry at her, lunge at her, or, perhaps hardest of all, leave whenever she appeared. But she always loved him, even when it wasn't reciprocated (or so it seemed). That Christmas, when Abby did receive a note from Andrew, it put all of that to rest. She read Andrew's words aloud:

D E A R A B (a short-form term of endearment that only a handful of people use with Abby—randomly and inconsistently—but clearly enough that Andrew picked it up). She read it and looked up at me, eyes wide, as if to say "Mom, did he really mean to write that?" And, of course, he did; he stopped at A, B, and then continued on to the next word. It was very touching to witness. She continued reading:

I LOVE YOU. I CANNOT THINK OF MY LIFE WITHOUT YOU IN IT. YOU ARE VERY SPECIAL TO ME. WE ARE UNITED.

Even for a little girl of only eight, she was clearly moved. Taking it in, she looked up with a soft smile, beaming. She had heard his words, words meant just for her. She felt his love. We all did, in that moment. It was one of the most beautiful gifts I had ever seen exchanged.

Years later, Abby described what having a brother like Andrew was like. She was eleven. I had asked her to do a little video that I could share with others through *Life, Love & Autism*.

"One part of it is awesome because you know a different side of someone that no one else would know. Maybe other people my age who don't have that experience would most likely be scared or anxious or nervous. There's an element of greatness that comes with Andrew being my brother. Sometimes it's hard, sometimes it's embarrassing, like walking down the street, everyone's staring at Andrew, or when my school friends see him rummaging through the trees . . . but at the end of the day, I love him so much."

Although it took years for their relationship to grow into what it is now, their connection was there from the start. I'll never forget the day I caught both of them sitting together at the kitchen counter in complete and comfortable silence. That moment really struck me: these two souls had gotten to know each other on a level beyond words.

Andrew later wrote: A BEAUTIFUL EXPERIENCE IS TO BE ABLE TO HAVE SOMEONE BE WITH ME IN MY SILENCE. MANY PEOPLE USE TOO MANY WORDS WHEN THEY COULD ACTUALLY SAY MORE WITH LESS. THERE IS COMFORT IN FILLING SPACE WITH WORDS. SILENCE IS VERY UNCOMFORTABLE FOR SOME. MAYBE IT IS WORTH SPENDING SOME TIME THERE.

Abby does that for Andrew. She can be with him in all of who he is, in all of who *she* is, and say nothing. Abby regularly shows us what unconditional love looks like. She will forever be Andrew's ally, his greatest defender, his biggest fan. Hers is an other-centered love; she, so deserving of that love herself.

Abby is *intentional* with life, finding joy and connection in the present moment. She reminds me to have fun; she and her dad are *both* good at that. There is so much I would miss, so much joy I wouldn't see or hear, if it weren't for Abby. I worry less now, under the layers of life's busyness, about whether I've paid enough attention or spent enough quality time with Abby. She knows my heart. Abby is my forever reminder of the light that comes after dark.

"ALL THAT MATTERS
IS LOVE."
—ANDREW

CHAPTER 26

James died when Andrew was two, before Abby was born. One of the most profound losses of my life and one I reflect on every year on James's birthday. I had never reflected, though, on what that loss might have been like for Andrew; Andrew had lost his brother.

Andrew and I had been answering some questions on his letterboard for school, questions about life and what makes him who he is. In an unintended moment, I turned to him and said, "Andrew, I've never asked you about this . . . It's a very special memory and you're a very intuitive and connected kid." He was thirteen at the time.

He looked at me with direct eye contact, looked away, then looked back. He knew I was speaking right to him.

"Do you think we could take a minute to talk about Baby James?"

We had been allowed to have immediate family into the NICU where James had been living. My in-laws, who had been taking care of Andrew while Stuart and I lived there with James, brought Andrew in to see us and to meet James, his little brother. Andrew, an active toddler, hovered thoughtfully over James's little bed: James, covered in tubes, Andrew, not yet speaking, not yet diagnosed with autism.

"You met him. You were very little, Andrew. I want to ask you: Do you have any thoughts on what James meant to our family? On what he meant *for* our family?"

My heart started racing as Andrew carefully spelled out:

WOULD YOU AGREE THAT IT BROUGHT YOU AND DAD CLOSER TOGETHER? AND THAT IT TAUGHT YOU HOW STRONG YOU ARE AND HOW SUPPORTED YOU ARE. AND THAT IT SHOWED DAD HOW CAPABLE HE IS OF EXPERIENCING SUCH DEEP FEELINGS AND BEING BRAVE. JAMES HAD A SPECIFIC ROLE TO PLAY IN YOUR GROWTH AS A SOUL AND FOR HIS OWN SOUL'S GROWTH.

His words took my breath away. On some level, I knew Andrew would have wisdom around it, though I wasn't sure what would come forward; he hadn't been spending much time with me on the letterboard in those days.

"Do you remember meeting him?" I was curious.

NO, BUT MY SOUL DOES. I KNEW HE WAS COMING . . . (tears start in my eyes as I watch these words spell out before me)...TO BE HERE WITH US AND I KNEW IT WOULD BE HARD I JUST DIDN'T KNOW THE DETAILS. I KNEW WHAT HE WAS COMING HERE TO HELP YOU LEARN. WE ARE ALL IN THIS TOGETHER. WE HELP EVOLVE EACH OTHER'S SOULS. YOU GAVE HIM THE SOUL EXPERIENCE OF A PHYSICALLY BURDENED LIFE TO LEARN THAT WE ARE TRULY MOST ALIVE AS SOULS IN SPIRIT BEYOND THIS PHYSICAL LIFE.

I could hardly read the words I had scribed in front of me, my eyes were so welled up with tears.

Andrew got upset at this point in his writing. Perplexed, I asked, "This is hard?"

And he responded, BECAUSE YOU HAVE NEVER ASKED ME ABOUT THIS BEFORE AND IT IS VERY HARD TO PUT INTO WORDS. I agreed with him. It absolutely is.

Andrew is just so smart, so connected. I forget this sometimes when Andrew *looks* disconnected (to us). In fact, he is connected to a very deep, very meaningful place—far more meaningful than where most of us allow ourselves to go. Is this because of his autism? It is because of who he is—deeply soulful, deeply connected to wisdom and truths beyond this world. Perhaps *because* he is autistic, we stop to listen and marvel at his words more than if they came from you or me (or someone we might *expect* to write such words). "We are all in this together. We help evolve each other's souls." These are words I've learned from deeply spiritual people. *How does Andrew know these deep truths?* Somehow, I knew he would.

I was in awe. To be honest, I was moved and grateful. I wasn't sure what was more meaningful: seeing how beautifully connected Andrew is in his own life or having been given the opportunity to revisit this part of mine.

"Are you connected now?" I asked.

OF COURSE. HE IS ONE OF MY BEST FRIENDS.

I laughed. "Can you tell him I say hi?" I knew what Andrew would say.

YES, BUT SO CAN YOU.

Andrew is so wise; we *are* all connected. James, Andrew, Abby, Stuart, and me. All of us—our families, our friends, our communities.

Stuart and I grew together, in love and strength and partnership, through James, because of James. This journey, albeit full of bumps and turns, has brought Stuart and me closer. We have seen each other in our lowest lows and through the highest highs.

I laugh, thinking back to when Stuart and I first met. Rose-colored glasses, full of fun, ambition, and outlook:

Where will we travel? Who will be at our wedding? How many children will we have?

We had no idea that the love we fell into would lead us through a deeply transformative journey; it would lead us to exactly who we were meant to become as individuals and as a couple based in love.

PART IV: AWAKEN

"IF EVER YOU FORGET WHO YOU ARE,
GO BACK INTO NATURE
AND YOU WILL FIND YOURSELF AGAIN."
-ANDREW

CHAPTER 27

Surrender would continue to be my lifelong pursuit. Being open to the process of life, including that which I couldn't control, while trusting in *possibility*–this had become my life's experiment. I was getting multiple opportunities to practice personally, but this next one had the whole family involved. This next one was big. I remember saying, "How bad does it have to get before we decide to make a change?" This was that point.

It all began at the start of the year, a dark, gray January. Andrew was having an increasingly difficult time at the autism center (one we were trying out closer to home), head-banging into walls and doors resulting in excessive nosebleeds, which culminated in one particular escalated incident when Andrew's head broke through a classroom door. That was it–I pulled him out of school, out of the center, out of everything; it was down to ground zero.

We hired 1:1 partners. He spent more time outside, hiking and biking. His dysregulation (and nosebleeds) decreased. Still, there was an anxiety in Andrew that was constant. I threw out all sorts of ideas, from medication to functional nutrients to service dogs. While Andrew's state calmed over time (CBD and nutrients had an impact), the idea of a service dog stuck; a steady, regulating influence never left my mind. I researched autism service dog organizations, put us on wait lists (of one to two years), and secretly mentioned it to a few friends (secretly, as in I didn't want Abby to find out as she'd be relentless, nor Stu as he'd be totally opposed). It was just *an idea.*

And that's when we lost Andrew. At that point, I vowed to get a dog. I was exhausted from a particularly stressful week and calling 911 for my lost nonspeaking son had me hit bottom. I decided I needed a companion. (And yes, Andrew would benefit too.) I felt desperate. One friend connected me with a woman in the neighborhood who trained guide dogs for CNIB Foundation (an organization supporting Canadians who are blind or living with vision loss)—even just for me to be able to ask a few questions about the process of bringing a service dog into the home. She was a wonderful resource and, in fact, opened her home to us so that Andrew and I could meet the black lab retriever she was training at the time. Not only would I see what Andrew was like with a dog but I could also test him for allergies by getting him to touch, smell, and breathe it all in.

The neighbor mentioned that many of the guide dogs being trained for service don't pass their program: they are either too friendly, not willing to work, or, in the case with this dog, they eat socks! Sometimes these "second-career dogs" are adopted into families with disabilities *other than* vision loss. Such would be the case with Murdoch, the dog she was currently training. If we were keen, she was happy to put our name forward to CNIB Guide Dogs. I agreed.

I told Abby; I couldn't help it. I told her I wasn't promising anything, and that we would have to educate (convince) Stu, but something felt right. And not just with a companion dog in general, but with Murdoch. Murdoch lived in our neighborhood, he was great with kids, he had been to Quebec a number of times (specifically to where we were spending more and more time as a family), and loved to be active and outdoors. It seemed like a perfect fit.

Abby and Stuart met Murdoch. We invited Murdoch over just to see what having a dog in our backyard was like. It was lovely to see Abby playfully interacting, Stu observing (he did not grow up around dogs), and Andrew timid but tolerant. Murdoch had a beautiful way of gently following Andrew around the yard while also giving him space.

We asked Andrew, "What was it like for you, having Murdoch around?"

He wrote: IF A DOG WOULD HANG OUT WITH ME THE WAY MURDOCH DID, I WOULD FEEL LIKE I HAD A FRIEND. MURDOCH DIDN'T HESITATE. HE DIDN'T NEED TO BE ENCOURAGED TO HANG WITH ME. HE LIKED ME FOR ME. HOW GREAT TO HAVE A BUDDY LIKE THAT.

It was actually quite something to watch. I think it's what sold us.

Months went by. We didn't hear anything. We hadn't been offered Murdoch. We practiced surrender and trust; if he was meant for us, it would happen. We learned that Murdoch had been registered for a trial with another family. Our hearts sank—clearly a sign that we were invested. That trial fell through, however, and shortly thereafter, we got an email from CNIB Guide Dogs requesting an interview with our family. By the end of the summer, we were offered a two-week trial with Murdoch, the dog from down the street that Andrew and I had met a mere three months prior.

What I didn't foresee was the intense personal examination I would undergo. Layers would be peeled back and deep digging abounded, all in a two-week trial of a dog.

We were happy to welcome Murdoch into our home, albeit a bit nervous. This was all new for Stu, and although I had grown up with a black lab (coincidentally) in the family, it had been decades prior. Abby was the most comfortable, hugging and loving Murdoch right away. Andrew was guarded. Interestingly, I noticed my anxiety rise as I watched puddles of drool and piles of black hair accumulate. This big, hairy, friendly dog was *a lot* to manage. I was grateful that the purpose of the trial was to see if this was a fit for our family. Because maybe it wasn't.

That same week, Andrew woke up with a raised red mark on his neck, right by his cheek. Odd. Within a few days, it had spread to his entire neck, face, and eyes. He looked inflamed. And then it hit me: he was reacting to the dog. Shoot, now what? We watched the rash for a few more days, but by week two, it seemed clear that this was not going away. The dog would have to go. Abby would be devastated. Stu, who had grown quite fond of Murdoch, might be too.

Meanwhile, I was seeing the drool, and the hair, and the dog toys, and I was secretly relieved that we had an out. I had become so anxious over the decision to keep this dog that I wasn't sleeping, and so when Andrew's rash presented, my whole body relaxed as I had a reason to say no. Only, Andrew wasn't allergic to the dog. One night, after his bath, I noticed Andrew's rash along his legs. It was oddly familiar. It reminded me of a rash I had had when I was Andrew's age. That was it! This was poison ivy. Okay, great, but . . .

I had already delivered the news to the family that we were not keeping Murdoch. Everyone was sad, even Stu. We had been preparing to say goodbye when I got confirmation that Andrew's rash was, in fact, poison ivy. This was no longer an easy out for Mom. I confided to Stu, who was not a "dog person," and who likes to maintain his things, and who is triggered by any destruction of property (as he calls it), about how I was hesitant to keep Murdoch. "Nope," he said. "I love this dog. This is on you, Susan." I was shocked at Stuart's transformation. *So what was my problem then?*

And that's when the self-discovery started.

I had grown accustomed to living in a clean, tidy home (which was unlike the home I had grown up in; this was how *Stuart* was raised, and in the end, I liked how it made me feel—like I was in control). Living in a home with a dirty, hairy dog seemed like a bad idea. What worried me more, though, was how Stu had shifted, saying things like "Well maybe this is going to lighten *me* up a bit, help me relax into a new version of myself." *What? Who is this person?* I was afraid that, in one years' time or five years' time, I was going to take the brunt when the truth of having a dog became apparent. "Who convinced me to have a dog! There's hair everywhere!" Stu might say. And I would agree.

That's when it all became clear to me.

There was fear and insecurity in this decision. I could not predict the future, let alone control it.

Do I fear the responsibility of having a dog? I wondered. Will dog hair and drool leave me feeling "out of control"? What am I trying to control, anyway? Stu? Our life? A tidy home?

I had spent years, especially once autism showed up, trying to control the things I could in order to feel good, to feel safe. Because then maybe I could manage okay with the things I *couldn't* control. A dog allergy or a husband who didn't want a hairy home were both excellent outs, which now I no longer had.

Awareness is always the first step.

I said yes. I bravely chose this as an opportunity to practice letting go. To relax a bit into a life that had black dog hair on white sweaters, along with loyalty, fun, and companionship. Maybe to relax a bit more in general.

Andrew *called it*. When we asked him during the trial how our family would benefit, he wrote:

YOU ALREADY KNOW ALL THIS, MOM.

But I persisted. "Tell me what you think, Andrew!"

Andrew continued on his letterboard: A FRIEND FOR ABBY. A COMPANION FOR ALL OF US. A LAUGH FOR DAD. LOVE AND WARMTH FOR YOU, MOM. THERE MIGHT BE A KINDNESS AND PLAYFULNESS IN THE HOUSE THAT WASN'T THERE BEFORE. HE IS SOFTENING THINGS IN OUR HOME WITH HIS LOVE.

And he was right. Murdoch *was* softening things. Coy, Andrew ended with: PLUS, HE IS A SUPER HANDSOME GUY LIKE ME.

We laughed. Abby added: "I love him so much. I loved him right when I met him. I would love for him to be our dog!"

So, now there's Murdoch. The ultimate experiment in surrender.

So thrilled with having Murdoch as our pet, Abby (a creative, born entrepreneur) chose to donate 10 percent of sales from her thriving Abby's Joy bracelet business to CNIB Guide Dogs. All on her own volition. Abby continues to impact the lives of many, just as Andrew does.

www.abbysjoy.ca

"AWARENESS IS ALWAYS
THE FIRST STEP."
-SUSAN

CHAPTER 28

Over all the years when I thought I was losing myself, I was, in fact, finding me.

Early motherhood (probably motherhood in general) reduced me to an identity that was one of caregiver, laborer, chef, chauffeur, health consultant, and appointment coordinator; essentially, a family's project manager. In there I had forgotten who I was. "Am I even fun? I used to be fun!" I would say, half-jokingly.

I am fun. Yes, I had maintained my nutrition passion, my close groups of friends, and my tenaciousness, but finally, after more than a decade of other-centered love and service as a mother, I was finding fun and joy in *me* again. It had always been there–kind of like the sun: clouded over on some days, especially when it's stormy, but still there. Same with Stu and me: our capacity for laughter, conversation, intimacy–it never really went away; it was just dampened by some rainy days.

Believing that my children, especially my nonspeaking autistic son, could be cared for by people other than me was one of the hardest but most significant pieces to my happiness and wholeness as a person–as a human being and as a mother.

With a fresh autism diagnosis and a newborn baby in my arms, and while still grieving the loss of a child, in those days, I had no choice; to survive, I had to accept help. There was one time, when Andrew was very young and in a particularly tough stage, where I arrived to my in-laws' house, threw my hands up, and said, "*You* deal with him! I can't do this any longer!" And they did. I was lucky to have them, not everyone does, because for me, it was more the lesson of learning that, *regardless* of how he was taken care of, I needed it. I needed the relief. And I needed to do that for myself in order to do that for my children.

Yes, there is always the "risk" that leaving my child in the hands of someone else may result in a *more* dysregulated, more upset child (which could negate any respite I may have achieved, and where I would have to undo any damage to my child). But for that moment in time (and I had to coach myself in the actual moment), it was worth it. It was necessary. It became essential to my well-being.

I let grandparents drive Andrew to his outdoor preschool. I let neighbors take him for walks. I let friends hold Abby so I could bake, clean, rest.

And it got easier.

I could leave Andrew and Abby for a weekend away with Stu—even when it meant coming home to a household unraveled.

We could go out to a neighborhood party, leaving the children with a sitter—even when it meant coming back to an overflowing toilet, flooded ceiling, and a smashed lamp.

I could send Andrew to school, knowing he would sometimes be upset but would be looked after, so that I could write this book and have my own time.

For in each of these moments, it was worth it—even when it meant having to deal with any repercussions.

Why is it so hard? Because no one does it like a mother, like a parent who knows their child's needs even before they do. Because knowing this means we can anticipate upsets before they happen. Then we can control for that. And then maybe, if we can control for all things, maybe everything will be okay. Maybe our child will be content. Maybe our environment will stay sane. Maybe *we* will be okay. It makes perfect sense. It also makes for a hypervigilant, raw and spent human, which is why, years ago, I had to learn to let go.

I had to learn that, in order for me to live, I had to let my children live too. For me to grow, to flourish even, I had to let them step into the world. To get hurt, dirty, and to risk it all—to risk everything that I had controlled for. It is through risk and vulnerability that we find courage. And *that's* how it gets easier. That's "all" it takes.

Even Abby agrees, though she is the cautious and aware big little sister who knows that only Mom and Dad do it best. She still knows that it is of benefit to have Andrew learn to receive care from others, and certainly, that it benefits her mom and dad.

What does Andrew think? When I shared my thoughts with him, he wrote:

OF COURSE THIS IS ALL TRUE. BUT IN LETTING OTHERS INTERACT WITH MY WORLD, WE ARE TEACHING OTHERS HOW TO INTERACT WITH MY WORLD. THUS BEGINS THE RIPPLE.

It was all true. Andrew's words, my words, our story—a true story of love, loss, perseverance, faith, trust, triumph, joy, magnificence, and letting go. Who would have thought, all these years later, I would be using his words to inspire mine.

You could say to me that there is more to life and love and autism than words, and I would agree with you. Andrew would agree with you! But what I've learned through this journey, *because of* this journey, and because of Andrew's life through spelling to communicate, is this:

There is clearly so much we do not know about the autistic mind—and about human potential, in fact—if we did not know *this*! Nonspeaking autistic individuals are teaching us that there is more to learning and thinking and to the experience of being human than we ever knew. Andrew himself writes about being able to access higher level thinking. He calls it "universal knowledge"—something we all have access to, he says (and notes that he will share more in the book he wants to write). Andrew is not alone. I have met more autistic minds tuned into this level of thinking, this depth of wisdom, this rich sense of beauty, than can *just* be a coincidence. I believe Andrew and others are here to bring humanity to a higher place of knowing and of being. Ultimately, to a place of love.

Through this journey I have learned how important it is to question convention, to question what we're told, to question the status quo. What if I had never wondered what else was out there for Andrew, for me, or for our family? What if I had never questioned "the experts"? Get curious. Wonder. Be brave. Look outside the box. Then tune in. We are the true experts on ourselves and our children. No one knows better. We must trust that. Our instincts, our intuition and our knowing (and not just in the ethereal sense, but literally, what we actually *know*) are there to provide us with insight and direction. An internal compass. We must learn to trust ourselves enough to be guided.

The letterboard to me became a symbol of exactly these things. Of what happens when we are open to life's possibilities, and when we trust ourselves enough to take the road less traveled. A sign that solutions don't always come in the form we expect. An example of what it looks like to let go of expectations and outcomes. For me, the letterboard is a true testimony of what happens when we surrender.

Through this journey I have learned to be gentle with myself, forgiving, and compassionate. I have learned that none of us are alone. Connecting with others through my writing has given validation to this journey—mine and thousands of others walking a similar path. Each story, part of something bigger. A story of love and family, perseverance and triumph, all of it became part of the human experience that we share. The experience of learning to let go, of being open, and of trust. I have learned that this is where the possibilities exist and where the extraordinary happens.

In what felt like a reckoning, I received my own note from Andrew one Christmas. We were creating cards for family members when I asked him if there was anyone else to whom he'd like to write. Y O U, he wrote.

As I watched his words unfold, letter after letter, I felt a wave of warmth come over me.

His words read:

MOM, FEELING OVERCOME WITH A BEAUTI-FUL FEELING OF LOVE AND GRATITUDE FOR YOU AND ALL YOU HAVE DONE FOR ME ALL THESE YEARS. I AM FOREVER GRATEFUL. HOW YOU HAD THE PATIENCE AND PERSEVERANCE IS A GIFT I WILL KEEP CLOSE IN MY HEART ALWAYS. HERE'S TO SO MUCH AHEAD FOR US.

I was moved to tears. My dear sweet Andrew.

What I have gained over these years is something that, ironically, is hard to put into words: Personal insight and opportunities for growth that many people wait a lifetime for. All of it, every hardship and every triumph, bringing me to this present moment in time, exactly where I was always meant to be.

I told him this. He smiled, gazing just past my face into the distance.

Then I asked him about the letter. The letter I had written the day I exploded, many years before. The letter I had written to my autistic child and the note I imagined he would write me in return. In many ways, he had just written me that note—about love and forgiveness and courage. But I asked him anyway. I read him the letter. And then I held up the letterboard for his reply.

YES, MOM, ALL I SAW WAS LOVE.

"WE NEED TO REMEMBER
THAT WE ARE POWERFUL.
WE HOLD THE ABILITY
TO CREATE A BEAUTIFUL WORLD."
-ANDREW

CHAPTER 29

Just when I thought the book had been written, another chapter appeared. This was an important one—one just for me. The one on stillness. The one where I would enter a spiritual transformation I could no longer resist. I admit, it wasn't stunning. A well-intended escape into nature for recalibration and pause became a messy soulful teardown until, ironically, there was nothing left but to be still. No doubt, that was its purpose from the beginning. A call to show up in a different way—beyond surrender. (Surrender, I could do; surrender was action-oriented, at least, just in the act of *having to* surrender.)

A call into stillness.

It was spring. Coming out of winter was grueling; it often is, with Andrew. Like spring itself, there is an emergent energy, an energy bursting to break free from the indoors, from the gray, with a desire to take up space. But *this particular* spring felt more like a "ping-pong" type energy—seeing it in Andrew, in our household, and then seeing it in myself. An exhausting energy.

I was getting calls from Andrew's school that he was struggling: he was biting his shirt and banging his head, flipping desks and dumping garbage bins. It was the same at home. Andrew was all over the house and getting into things, undoing bins of mitts and hats, searching for pleasurable "flickers" (items he could flick and listen to by his ear), be it house plant leaves or tissues, and coming in and out of the house, in and out, through the back door. He couldn't sit still. Meanwhile, I was in the thick of writing this book. Here I was, trying to enjoy the process of writing, when really, I felt stretched and spent. I was irritable and impatient. I practiced self-care: tea chats and dinner with friends, attending dance classes, sharing soulful texts with other moms who were experiencing similar things with their children. But our homelife was awful. Life felt unpredictable. Something had to shift.

I decided I would take Andrew out of school and into the forest.

For a few years, by this point, we had been spending time as a family in a quiet place in the forests of Quebec. We bought a place in the woods where we could enjoy fun in the summer and activities in the winter. Year round we enjoyed its tranquility, a place of respite and retreat, including for Andrew. Typically, the moment we arrive, our bodies relax, and any stress washes away. We fall into *simple living* with lots of time outside, enjoying the beauty of nature. My thought was that we would go to our place, Andrew could "just be," and I would write. Just the two of us. Even just for a few days.

Only it didn't go like that.

Andrew was agitated and jumpy, leg-slapping, head-banging, upset. Throwing things and dumping things. Nonstop movement—constant—except in sleep. Music had to be off, and he had no tolerance for my laptop being out. The vision I had of me writing my book while Andrew enjoyed being in the trees vanished. Eventually, even my phone was a trigger. If I held it, Andrew would push it away. If I was sending a text, he would vocalize "nah" and get upset—maybe bang his head or bite his shirt. His body was unsettled and tense. I could grab a photo here or there, but eventually, I was limited to very little, save for the sounds and emptiness of the space around us.

And there it was. Right in front of me. The initial call to stillness. And I was still missing it. In truth, I was resisting it.

Those three days were suffocating. I was at a loss with no idea where to go. I felt angry and sad, discouraged and depleted. At one point, watching Andrew forcefully bang his head against a tree, I looked up through the forest canopy and yelled, "What the f*ck!" Tears overtook me. I gave up.

It felt all too familiar. Hadn't we gone through this before? Weren't we over these ups and downs? In the past we would seek Andrew's input, something that offered us insight and even solutions for how to help him, how to better understand. But in those days, Andrew rarely spelled with me on the letterboard. If I offered, he pushed the letterboard away. Maybe he was done too. Deep down, somehow, none of this felt permanent; it felt transformative. That's when it hit a breaking point.

In one of Andrew's (or my) more dysregulated states, I felt a rage come over me where all I could do was breathe. Normally, I would have done a million other things—lose it, throw something, lunge forward—but, in that moment, all I could do was breathe. It was excruciating, actually painful. "Just breathe," something in me kept saying. And in a deep breath, still shaking, I steadily managed to say, "Andrew, what is going on! What happens to you?" I was exasperated.

I yelled. Then I breathed, and he breathed. I calmed a bit. He calmed a bit. He finally wrote: HOW DO I KNOW? MY BRAIN IS IN CHARGE AND IS OFTEN OUT OF BALANCE.

"What can I do to help you?" I managed to say.

BE MORE PATIENT THAN YOU ALREADY ARE.

I laughed, infuriated. "And where will I find more patience, Andrew?"

He looked at me and wrote on his letterboard:

IN THE STILLNESS OF YOUR CENTER. His words were poignant, and he meant it, but I was too upset to hear them. His words didn't land.

"But specifically, what does that mean!" I retaliated.

KEEP BREATHING AND ASKING FOR HELP.

"From where?" I implored.

FROM SOURCE WITHIN YOURSELF.

And I was speechless. I softened. He softened. I took a deep breath.

From source within myself. In the stillness of my center. It's what I needed to hear and I knew it. Maybe not consciously, but on some level, I had always known. A reconnection with the wisdom within. For years, years of running and responding and vigilance, I had been craving stillness, and for years, it was always right there, but I turned away. There was no turning away this time. My child, my nonspeaking autistic child, was mirroring what I needed: to just breathe, and to be still, because it was what *he* needed too. He wasn't like this with Stuart, though. This lesson was for me. It was standing right in front of me.

The book could wait. As Andrew told me with his letterboard: THE BOOK IS BEING WRITTEN.

***

I put the book on hold. It no longer felt like a priority (in fact, it felt like "pushing"). Nothing felt like a priority except learning how to be still. Plus, I wanted answers. I wanted someone to tell me what I needed to know to help Andrew. I wanted guidance. I needed "wisdom from above!" Perhaps I was still ignoring the wisdom from within.

I reached out to an intuitive (a spiritual sage) who said, "It's in the moments of silence that the purity of your connection with Andrew and the purity of your connection within yourself can be revealed. The real purity of your truth and light will not be able to be amplified until you drop in and surrender to the quiet."

She said what Andrew had been showing me: Be still. Breathe. Listen.

"This is going to change everything," she told me.

For me, it wasn't about trusting her words over my own knowing (though, for millennia, people have sought the wisdom of sages, shamans, prophets, mystics, guides, psychics, and intuitives–people with a deep spiritual connection), but about taking those words as wisdom, *knowing* they resonate with the truth of my own experience.

I'm still working out what stillness means for me: "dropping in," moving from my head to my heart, and listening, *actually listening*, to the voice within. It's not easy–the learning, the resistance, the doubt:

I don't know how to do it. It won't work for me. It won't work with Andrew (or Abby, or Stu). It's not working. It's not me. Autism requires more than this. I need to be doing more, something else. This is not enough.

Exhausting. But it was just the beginning. I committed to believing that the results would come. And then, things started to shift. I could feel it. I could see it in my life. I asked Andrew.

He wrote: I AM BETTER AS JUST YOU ALONE ARE BETTER.

In stillness, I can tune into the insight and the answers that may help me help Andrew—be it guidance for programs, people, places, therapies, or remedies.

In stillness, I am learning to drop into my heart. The more I connect with my heart, the more I can connect with Abby; this is the place where she lives.

In stillness, when it's working for me, it's working for Stu. He has long begged me to *just be*. "What are you doing that you're so busy?" he would say. Never about family life or house stuff—that, he gets; he's busy too. *About presence*. Being. Maybe he knew I'd find my way.

I was worried this would change me. I love the passionate, active, busy girl that I am. Stillness just shows me that I can operate in a different framework. Still loving all that I am and all that I *do*, just with a little more *be*.

And so, I practice. Every morning, before the household wakes, I take my morning journal and a tea to a quiet spot (usually outside where I can put my bare feet on the earth), and I sit. I breathe. I write my daily gratitudes, intentions, and affirmations. Then I close my journal and my eyes and I drop in. At first, it felt contrived: *Okay, Susan, follow your breathing, then listen . . .* Now, I just breathe. I let whatever comes up, come up: thoughts, words, to-do's. (If they're really persistent, I write them down so I can let them leave my mind.) And I come back to my breath, until eventually, a calm takes over. My thoughts slow, my body relaxes.

At first, my mind would screech: *This is so unproductive!* I knew to expect this. I would breathe into the discomfort and trust it would dissipate (although some days I would get up and leave as I couldn't stand my own inner wrestling). Eventually, I started to miss the mornings when I *didn't* sit in stillness. My day felt less "anchored"; I felt less present. Some days I would force myself to sit, even just for five minutes, so I could shift from anxiousness to presence. I would marvel at the simplicity of this tool, acknowledging how I had resisted it all those years. It had come at the perfect time.

One morning not long after, while sitting in stillness, I had a rush of words flood my mind. It was the morning after Andrew's fifteenth birthday. I heard the words, but urged them to go, to leave me in my stillness. They wouldn't let up. Instead of resisting, I took note. In fact, I wrote them down. They were statements, a story unfolding. With the household still asleep, I took that Sunday morning to capture the words I had been hearing in my head. The words flew from my fingertips. I needed only an hour, and when I was done, I had tears in my eyes. The story was true in every sense of the word.

Through the practice of stillness, a practice Andrew himself had shown me, one of the most powerful, impactful stories of Andrew's life had been written. The story of Andrew buying a new pair of shoes on his fifteenth birthday. I shared it to *Life, Love & Autism* that Sunday morning.

This is one of those stories where what you choose to do in that one split second changes the trajectory of someone else's life.

After a sleepy Saturday morning on Andrew's fifteenth birthday, I whisk him off to do a quick errand, just down the street. He needs summer sandals. We know the exact style and size, and go right when the store opens. We prefer to go when it's not busy.

"Size forty-one of those black slip-on sandals, please," I announce.

Andrew swiftly slips his socked feet into the shoes, with no protest, head-banging, or distress (as in the past)-a perfect fit. We box them up, pay, and I thank the two staff members who helped us on that quiet morning.

As we head toward the door, I say, "It's Andrew's birthday today. Fifteen! Got our new shoes and now we're off to celebrate with family." They reply, "Oh, happy birthday! That's great, have fun!"

What happens next only happens when you act on intuition. When you listen to the voice inside that says to stop and do it differently.

Instead of dashing out the door, I pause. And instead of making Andrew quickly point to the "thank you" symbol on his picture chart, I stop. I hold up his letterboard instead.

For ten years we have carried around a rudimentary picture chart-a compilation of words with symbols and pictures for Andrew (and anyone he's with) to quickly reference as a means to communicate. It contains his most important and most used words: people, places, food, greetings, and activities. Neighborhood kids, friends, cousins, and classmates have studied its pictures over the years, flipping through the extra strips at the top of the chart that contain even more "representations" of Andrew's life. This chart gets banged around, dirty, thrown, lost, found, and replaced over the years. Andrew also uses an iPad with a text-to-voice output app that conveys his needs and wants, again, through words with picture symbols. These tools offer Andrew the simplest, quickest way to communicate. But, of course, they are limited to just that.

Years ago we were introduced to a method that uses spelling on a letterboard to communicate. Simple but profound, this tool gives Andrew access to an effective and reliable means of conveying more than just his basic needs and wants. Having decided we should be carrying around his letterboard, too, we affixed a version of it to the back of his picture chart. No more fumbling with multiple charts and boards; now it was all in one place with a carrying strap. Brilliant.

But we must offer it to Andrew for him to use it; letterboard initiation is not automatic for him. As his parents, we need to remember to offer, take the time, and then respect Andrew's wishes if he pushes it away. (It requires significant time and effort for Andrew too.) We persevere because we know it gives Andrew an opportunity to share far more of who he is than can be conveyed through basic pictures and words.

And so I offered it to him.

I held up the letterboard on the back of his picture chart and I asked him to reply. He wrote, pointing to each letter, one by one: THANK YOU. And that was that.

We never know what the receivers of Andrew's words are thinking-what they make of it-while he is writing. We're so focused in that moment on all that goes into "spelling to communicate" using the letterboard-the regulation, the concentration, the transcribing. But it is always worth it.

I could tell the store staff were quiet, watching. When we looked up, they were stunned. I smiled and turned to leave.

"Um, can I ask you . . . What is that? How does he . . . What are you using there?" one store clerk, about my age, asked. "Because I have a brother-in-law . . . and he doesn't talk, but . . . "

And so it begins. This is what happens when we show up-in all of who we are-in our light, our strengths, and in our "deficiencies." We invite others into our humanness. And we allow them to share theirs.

"Oh! This is an alphabet board that Andrew uses to communicate. Right, Andrew? We've practiced it for years-it's quite incredible as we just didn't know Andrew was so "in there"-we didn't even know this tool existed-it's relatively uncommon, grassroots-but it's changed everything for us, for our family, for Andrew . . . "

I go on.

"Here. Let me write down a website, and my contact info, because it's always good to go through people who are actually using the method. And I can connect you with a local practitioner. Are you on Facebook? Because our family writes a blog and shares stories all about our journey . . . "

Of course, I ask the clerk about his brother-in-law. He is thirty, he doesn't talk but is able to do a lot for himself, on his own, but perhaps no one really knows him or much about him or what he knows. Maybe there's more there, the store clerk wonders. Maybe they could look into this . . .

"Amazing!" I say. "We've met people-haven't we, Andrew?-who were fifty and finally started using this method. What's your brother's name? Jason? Hey Andrew, what do you think? Maybe you have some words you want to share here?"

I quickly hold up the letterboard, concerned that our time might be running out, but Andrew very calmly and willingly starts pointing to letters:

TELL JASON . . .

And I immediately choke up. I forget, sometimes, just how powerful this tool is. Just how powerful Andrew is.

TELL JASON HE WILL CHANGE EVERYONE'S OPINION OF HIM IN TWENTY-SIX LETTERS.

We are all moved, awestruck, thrilled. "Wow," they say. "Thank you."

"I know!" I reply. Andrew smiles. "So, definitely reach out. Happy to connect. It really does change everything," I say.

And we leave. I am floating. And Andrew is singing (as he does).

This is how it happens-a movement. You start a

movement by vulnerably leading with your own life.
Maybe Jason and the store staff are reading this. I
hope so. I hope his whole family's life is changed
because Andrew showed up on his fifteenth birthday
to buy a pair of shoes.

The story reached thousands. Within an hour of being posted to *Life, Love & Autism*, hundreds had read Andrew's impactful words, and by the end of his birthday weekend, our "shoe store story" had been shared more than three thousand times from our humble blog, reaching tens of thousands of people across the globe. Hundreds of messages came in from those who had been touched by the story, including parents, friends, teachers, and caregivers of nonspeaking autistic loved ones. It would later be shared in *The Globe and Mail*, one of Canada's leading news outlets, as well as *Reader's Digest*, reaching thousands more. It is still the most shared story on our blog.

It had struck a chord. There was something about this story that spoke of the love we have for each other as humans. It brought up a feeling of happiness and warmth so deep that people felt moved to share it with others; people wanted others to feel what this story had brought up in them. A belief in the potential of others: the potential for growth, self-actualization, and impact. It was a story of hope, yes, and one of camaraderie (especially in the marginalized and underestimated), but it also gave testimony to the inherent human capacity to see greatness in others. It resonated so deeply because we know this to be true.

It took courage to submit our story—not because I doubted my words or didn't think it was a good read. It took courage because I didn't know where our story would land and I couldn't control that. There are naysayers, hard as that is to believe. Naysayers full of judgment, criticism, and doubt. In truth: the shadow side of us all, the shadow side of myself. The opposite of love and truth.

So, I sat with myself, right before I hit "publish," and I took a deep breath.

"I stand in the truth of who I am, of my story, of our family's story. And in standing in that truth, I trust that our words will go where they need to go, that they will land where they need to land, in the hands and hearts of those who need to hear them."

And that's exactly what happened.

Our family was proud of this story, proud of each other, and proud of Andrew. Proud of all of the years that led up to this story. When I showed Andrew the article in *The Globe and Mail*, complete with a sketch of him at the shoe store with his letterboard, he wrote:

I AM HAPPY THAT THE STORY WILL REACH MORE PEOPLE AND THAT THE LETTERBOARD MAY CHANGE MORE LIVES.

To which Stuart replied, "Even if just one other family's life is changed, you should feel so proud, Andrew."

Abby agreed. "I feel proud."

May we never underestimate the impact our story has on another. May we bravely show up in all of who we are. May we never dim our light. The world needs us.

"EVEN IF JUST ONE OTHER
FAMILY'S LIFE IS CHANGED . . . "
-STUART

CHAPTER 30

So here we are. More than a decade later, me, Stuart, Andrew, and Abby, and now Murdoch, standing in front of James's tree. Standing where we've stood so many times before. We have made a tradition of visiting James's tree every year, around the week of his birth or anniversary of his passing. Each time is different; some years are filled with sadness and grief, some years are quieter and more reflective, some years, we even forget–the date suddenly appearing in our calendar, reminding us to pause and remember.

This time it is neither momentous nor emotional. Nothing feels sad or hard or particularly joyous. But it is still noteworthy. This time there is a sense of *knowing* around us, like all the pages of our story, brimming with the wisdom that comes from having lived through each of the moments of our fifteen years together, they are all there before us. The pages written by us.

Imagine if we had known all of what lay ahead, the hardship and the challenge, but that *from* that, a beautiful life would unfold–that it had already begun–that it would be this life, a life full of growth and opportunity.

This time, visiting James's tree feels complete, whole. I, too, feel whole. That every piece of my story, Andrew, James, Abby, intentionally shaped who I was meant to become, who I am now. Stuart, too, our relationship, closer than it ever was before. Each a piece of the whole. I am who I am *because of* my life's experiences, not in spite of them. We all are.

I never knew possibility until I knew Andrew.

I never knew unconditional love until I held James.

I never knew joy until I lived life with Abby.

I never knew vulnerability until I walked in partnership with Stu.

I never knew all I didn't know until I fully surrendered to this life and watched it be revealed.

If we can trust it, life unfolds in mysterious and miraculous ways.

I see all of the growth in front of me: Andrew, fifteen years old, tall and self-assured, knowing who he is beyond words; Abby, beautiful and compassionate, with a genuine love of life and family; Stuart, steady in his support, love, and commitment to us; and James, his tree, magnificent and strong. Only recently did we—Abby, actually—realize that Andrew's favorite leaf, the oak leaf, stems from the tree that represents his brother. In Andrew's words: "strong, thick, unwavering." "So cool!" Abby exclaimed. "Andrew's favorite leaf is the same as James's tree!" Of course it was Abby making that beautiful connection between her two brothers.

So interesting, these moments that are full circle. The ones that bring us right back to where we started. The path that lies in front of us is now familiar, not just because we've walked it before, together, but because we know now who we are: a family rooted in love, each of us our own person, a collection of courage and humanness, with a deep knowing that love transcends all words.

I do not know where this story goes, what happens next, or how the story ends, but what I do know is this: There is a richness to be found in this life. It exists in the moments of joy that come out of pain. It is in the experience of triumph that comes through persevering. And it can be found in all of the possibilities that come from letting go. It is available to us when we allow ourselves to *be in it*. It's what life puts before us, beyond anything we could have imagined for ourselves when we first began. It is the story of our life.

This *is* that story, that life. One I am forever grateful for.

Truly, a life beyond words.

A FINAL WORD

I THINK MOST OF US WANT TO BELIEVE THAT OUR LIFE HAS PURPOSE. I KNOW THAT WHEN I WAS TRAPPED IN MY BODY AS A NONSPEAKING KID, I FELT LESS CONNECTED TO MY PURPOSE. WAS IT TO TEACH MY DAD PATIENCE? WAS IT TO TEACH MY MOM TO TRUST HERSELF MORE? WAS I GOING TO MAKE A DIFFERENCE? ONCE WE FOUND THE LETTERBOARD, I FOUND A GREATER CONNECTION TO MY PURPOSE, WHICH IS TO REMIND PEOPLE THAT LOVE IS ABOVE ALL THINGS. I THOUGHT I COULD COMMUNICATE THAT WITHOUT WORDS, BUT MANY PEOPLE DON'T PAY ATTENTION TO NONSPEAKING AUTISTIC KIDS SO I AM HAPPY TO USE THE LETTERBOARD. ENERGETICALLY, YOU CAN FEEL MY PURPOSE WITHOUT WORDS.

JUST BEING HERE MEANS OUR LIFE HAS PURPOSE. WE JUST FORGET. OF COURSE WE ALL WANT TO FEEL PURPOSEFUL, BUT OUR NUMBER ONE PURPOSE IS TO BE LOVE.

SO HOW CAN YOU SHOW UP AS LOVE IN YOUR LIFE? IS IT BEING LOVING TO SOMEONE WHO YOU FIND HARD TO LOVE? IS IT BY FORGIVING SOMEONE? WHAT ABOUT TO YOURSELF? HOW

DO YOU NEED TO LOVE YOURSELF MORE? HOW DO YOU NEED TO SHOW YOURSELF LOVE? ARE YOU HAPPY IN YOUR WORK? DOES YOUR WORK NEED TO CHANGE? CAN YOU BE MORE CREATIVE IN YOUR WORK? CAN YOU BE MORE CREATIVE IN YOUR LIFE? CAN YOU FIGURE OUT WHAT YOU LOVE AND DO MORE OF THAT BECAUSE THAT IS FULL OF FUN AND JOY AND CHARACTER UNIQUE TO YOU? AND THAT IS WHAT BRINGS MORE LOVE TO THE WORLD. AND THAT IS YOU LIVING YOUR LIFE WITH PURPOSE.

IF I CAN RIDE MY BIKE, EAT HEALTHY GOOD FOOD, AND SHARE MY WORDS WITH THE WORLD, THEN I FEEL I AM FULL OF PURPOSE AND THAT I AM BEING MY PURPOSE, WHICH IS TO BE ME.

—ANDREW, AGE 12
APRIL 2021

THANK YOU

To my mom and dad, Marg and Larry, thank you for the gift of my life. For all you taught me, through your example, on faith and trust and speaking one's truth. For teaching me to face hardship and embrace growth. For showing me that change is possible at any age. And for your constant encouragement. You two are my biggest cheerleaders. I am forever grateful.

To Susan and Lister, my parents-in-law, thank you for your generous spirit. Writing this book, pursuing my interests, taking breaks from life, none of it would have happened without you. You are incredible grandparents to my children and provide unwavering support to Stuart and me. We are truly thankful.

To our family—my sister Jayne, my brother John, my sister-in-law Sam, and to your partners and your children, for your support through the loss of James, and for your unconditional love of Andrew and Abby. You continue to reinforce for us the importance of family and of the gift that it is. To my aunts, Aileen and Elsie, for your support and praise, all these years.

To the people at Breakthrough Autism and Magnificent Minds— Alley, Nancy, Kristin, Melissa, Danielle, Zachary, Shawna, Kathleen, and Sandy—for all the learning in those early years. You gave us a platform from which to grow. To Kate, for being Andrew's friend. And to all of Andrew's therapists, teachers, and practitioners, it takes a village to empower a child and you are that village. To Natasha, Jillian, Tania, Kathleen, Paula, and Dr. Ostfield, for truly seeing Andrew.

To the letterboard community, the spellers and their parents and partners, Jordyn and Kelli, Giorgena and William, our greatest fan and ally Sherri, and all of our spelling friends and families—you continue to inspire this journey. And, of course, Elizabeth, who enhanced the nonspeaking landscape by giving us the tool of Spelling to Communicate. Our lives are forever changed.

To my team of teachers, guides, and therapists over the years—Dr. Barb, Dr. Ashit, Iva, Natalie, and Rachel—for your guidance and wise counsel. And, of course, Jade, who continues to do her work from above.

To the readers of our blog, *Life, Love & Autism*, for bearing witness to this journey and for supportively sharing our words with others. And to my fellow Canadian and British-language readers, thank you for tolerating the spelling and grammar of international publishing standards, knowing that neighbor, of course, includes a "u."

To all those who have been part of my writing journey—Tina, Ashley-Ann, Jazmin, Sabrina, Kelly, Christine, Michelle, and Sara—thank you for helping bring this story into the lives of others. To my early readers, Karin, Sherri, Helen, and Danielle, for your time and perspective. This book would not be what it is were it not for your insight. Estelle, for your design sense. And to my fellow authors, for your example.

To Julie and Helen, for encouraging me to share my words beyond what I could see in front of me, and for sharing Andrew's with the world. Thank you.

To my "mom friends"—each one of you in Thornhill and Toronto—thank you for being there for our family through our loss, thank you for planting James's tree, thank you for embracing our family into the lives of yours. This journey would have looked very different were it not for you. Thank you for the countless teas and drinks with friends; they carried me. A warm thank you to our neighbors, Deb and Greg, who lovingly watched Andrew explore their front garden, day after day, in those very early years of discovery.

To my "autism mom friends," for understanding without judgment or inquiry. For listening, laughing, and celebrating with me. For making it all feel okay. And to Karin, for making me feel like I was never alone.

To my nutrition friends and soul sisters—Melissa, Michelle, Corinne, Rose-Anne, Evelina, Kristina, Meredith, Nancy, Shawn, Ingrid, Lisa, Lianne, Lori, Caroline, Jenn, Laura, Julie, Meghan, Joy, Tia, Colleen, Jen, Nicole, and Melissa—for your perspectives and your light.

To my longtime friends, Michelle and Deana, and, of course, Fiona, for introducing me to Stuart. And to Katherine and Sean, for your marathon friendship. Thank you, each of you, for being there with us in the dark times, but mostly, for all of the good times and all of the laughs.

To those who know Stu: his childhood friends, neighborhood friends, friends of mine, colleagues, and his cycling community, and to Mike, who fits into all of those categories. Thank you for being an outlet. My hope is that you read this book and promise never to feel sorry for Stu. This is his story too.

To my children, for being who you are. Andrew, for coming into my life and making me a mother, and for showing me everything I needed to unlearn and relearn to truly understand life. Words will never convey how deeply you have changed my life; they don't have to. Abby, for the example you set of joy and fun and forgiveness. I am grateful for you every single day, every morning when you wake up, every day that you bounce down the stairs, every time you say I *love you*. You complete our family just by being you. And to James, for showing me what it looks like to truly live.

Finally, to Stuart, for your love, your friendship, your admiration, and for your constant support and commitment to our family. For never bringing work home, and for coming home, all those days when it might have been easier not to. For making us laugh and for bringing fun and possibility into our every day. From that very first time you and I visited the forests of Quebec, to where we are now, thank you for holding a vision of what life could include for our family, and for turning that vision into a reality. You have been instrumental in my personal growth; thank you for not being afraid to grow alongside me. To all of what's ahead. To you, to me, to us. I love you.

To life's mysteries, synchronicities, and to the process of living, I am forever in awe.

And to my spiritual anchor, Source, I am forever in gratitude.

Susan

RESOURCES

In order of mention:

More Than Words® program
www.hanen.org/Programs/For-Parents/More-Than-Words

Picture Exchange Communication System® (PECS®)
In Canada: www.pecs-canada.com/pecs
Global: www.pecsusa.com/our-offices

Language Acquisition through Motor Planning (LAMP)™
www.lampwflapp.com

Gut and Psychology Syndrome (GAPS) nutritional protocol
and diet
www.gaps.me
www.doctor-natasha.com

Canadian Adaptive Snowsports (CADS)
www.cads.ski

Track3: Ontario adaptive sports association
www.track3.org

Snow Valley Ski Resort, Barrie, Ontario
www.skisnowvalley.com

Holland Bloorview sibling support
www.hollandbloorview.ca/services/programs-services/
sibling-support-program

Spiral Praxis brain–body movement therapy
www.adaptedspiralpraxis.com

Spelling to Communicate (S2C™)
www.i-asc.org/s2c-spelling-to-communicate

International Association for Spelling as Communication
(I-ASC)
www.i-asc.org

Autism Canada
www.autismcanada.org

MedicAlert medical ID bracelets
www.medicalert.ca

CNIB GuideDogs
www.cnib.ca/en/programs-and-services/live/
cnib-guide-dogs

Additional resources:

Sherri Taylor
International Spelling to Communicate (S2C™)
virtual practitioner
sherri@spellersconnect.com

Jess Sherman
Supporting neurodivergent children through natural health
with a focus on nutrition.
www.jesssherman.com

Meredith Deasley
Supporting physical and emotional health of families and
children through nutrition and life coaching.
www.theresourcefulmother.com

Ashit Kapadia, Naturopathic Doctor, Classical Homeopath
mynaturopath@gmail.com

Colleen Lindberg, Intuitive
Instagram: @thecolleenlindberg

Dr. Danielle Ostfield, Clinical Psychologist
www.growingmindsto.ca

"Jordyn's Rocky Journey." YouTube. Adapted Spiral Praxis

"Andrew S. Life as a Nonspeaker." YouTube. Susan Baker

Recommended reading:

Bateson-Koch MD, Carolee. Allergies: *Disease in Disguise* (Alive Books, 1994)

Campbell-McBride MD, Natasha. *Gut and Psychology Syndrome (2nd edition)* (Medinform Publishing, 2010)

Cassotti, Consuelo. *Hearing a Different Voice* (Consuelo Cassotti, 2013)

Delahooke, Mona. *Brain-Body Parenting* (Harper, 2022)

Hall, Elaine. *Now I See the Moon* (Harper, 2010)

Handley, J.B. and Jamison Handley. *Underestimated: An Autism Miracle* (Skyhorse, 2021)

Herbert MD, Martha and Karen Weintraub. *The Autism Revolution* (Ballantine Books, 2013)

Higashida, Naoki. *The Reason I Jump* (Vintage Canada, 2016)

Kedar, Ido. *Ido in Autismland* (Sharon Kedar, 2012)

Libutti MD, Andrea. *Awakened by Autism* (Hay House, 2015)

Libutti MD, Andrea and João Carlos. *Autism: A New Perspective* (Independently published, 2019)

Miller, Suzy. *Awesomism! A New Way to Understand the Diagnosis of Autism* (iUniverse, 2008)

Ober, Clinton, Stephen T. Sinatra MD, and Martin Zucker. *Earthing (2nd edition)* (Basic Health Publications, Inc., 2014)

Peña, Diego M. *Anatomy of Autism* (CreateSpace Independent Publishing Platform, 2017)

Susan Baker is a passionate speaker, writer, and advocate. Featured on numerous family and personal growth podcasts, Susan shares her family's remarkable story of a profound communication breakthrough for their nonspeaking autistic son and the transformation that ensued. Combined with her background in holistic nutrition and education, Susan positively impacts others through her speaking engagements and social media presence on topics from health and nutrition, to living a purposeful life in the face of adversity. She is the author of *Life, Love & Autism*, an inspiring online blog that chronicles her family's journey through growth and challenge, including love, loss, and an autism diagnosis. Susan's words have reached thousands of households, from articles in *Reader's Digest* and *The Globe and Mail*—one of Canada's leading news outlets—to online parenting forums.

In addition to *A Life Beyond Words*, her first published book, she has coauthored two collaborations, *Lead with Love*, a collection of motherhood stories, and *For the Love of Our Children*, a holistic resource written *for* parents *by* parents of children with disabilities. She plans to coauthor a book with her nonspeaking son, Andrew, and she actively collaborates with Abby's Joy, her daughter's creative and charitable venture.

Susan lives in Toronto, Canada, with her husband Stuart, and their children, Andrew and Abby. They spend much of their time exploring the forests of Ontario and Quebec, including honoring the life of their child, James, with regular visits to the tree planted in his name.

For more stories, pictures, and inspiration, visit us at:

Facebook blog: *Life, Love & Autism*

Instagram: @lifewithsusan

Connect with Susan: susan@behealthyforlife.ca